Blogging

Unlock the Secrets to Making Your Blog Posts into Profit and Discover How Bloggers Make Money Online Utilizing Affiliate Marketing and Other E-Commerce Skills for Passive Income

Contents

Introduction

The following chapters will discuss the best secrets and strategies for becoming a pro-blogger and creating passive income. Making money online isn't something that only a select few special individuals get to do. You can do it too, as long as you have the drive and the information to do so.

The first stop along our journey will be looking at how people can blog for profit. The most important thing to figure out is if you are already a pro-blogger. Now, if you don't already have a blog, that's okay. In fact, it might be easier for you to become a pro-blogger because you are starting fresh. That doesn't mean, however, that you can't take an already formed blog and revamp it to make it profitable.

Then, we will move into the first blogging secret, which is content marketing. This means we will look at picking a niche, creating the best content, email marketing, and effective strategies. This is where everybody will have to start.

Then, we'll move into the second secret, which is affiliate marketing. This is the first way bloggers make money. Picking affiliate marketing networks can be hard to do, but we'll discuss how to pick the best, and how to be a market affiliate with Amazon.

Then, secret number three will discuss e-commerce and dropshipping. This is the second way you can make money with your blog. Selling products no longer means you have to have actual products on hand. Dropshipping has changed the game, and we will discuss the best way to use it.

Then, onto secret number four: expert information products. Much like the last secret, you will be selling a product, but this time it will be your expertise. This could mean writing a book, creating courses, or webinars.

Then, we will look at the last secret: advertising. This is a biggie, and something most people struggle with. It can be confusing to figure out how to advertise your blog or products, but it doesn't have to be. We will look at the best way to drive traffic to your site and to become a ninja at Google AdSense.

Chapter 1: Pro Blogging for Profit: How It's Really Done

You might not be new to the blogging game, but did you know that you can turn your blog into money? If you have thought about turning your blog into a professional blog, it could be the best decision you will ever make. You may not have even thought about professional blogging, but if you are brave enough to take a leap, it might make a new life for you. Don't get me wrong, being a professional blogger isn't easy. It takes time, knowledge, and skills to turn a blog into an income-generating, full-time job. Read on to find out more.

Are You a Pro Blogger?

Before you take that leap of faith, you have to understand that many things have changed over the past few years with blogging. Blogging isn't an easy and simple way to create income. But blogging is a very reputable way to make money online. If you commit to learning how to do it right and work hard, you can earn up to $1,000 a month with your blog.

You have to remember that when you want to make money by blogging, you have to approach and treat it just like a real business. Many bloggers have jumped into the river of professional blogging, however during the 2011 and 2012 Google Penguin and Google Panda updates, many blogs drowned. These bloggers decided to turn to other types of online marketing.

The reality is: if you don't stick with it, you are going to fail.

When making the decision to be a professional blogger full time, you have to consider many things, like your financial and social situation.

If you are single and don't have any family responsibilities, you might be able to handle all the risks. If you already have a full-time job that provides your family with security, you should first talk it over with everyone involved to see if taking that risk is worth it.

When you first start out blogging professionally, you need to figure out how many hours you can put into it. If you only have about three or four hours a day to commit to your blog, you might make about $400 to $500 a month. If you can work twelve to sixteen hours each day, you could increase your income drastically. If you have a family life, those hours might be too much for you to do.

Your income is going to come from sources like affiliate marketing, Google AdSense, direct ads, and other services. In order to be a successful professional blogger making a reliable income, you need to have certain skills.

You need to have professional skills in:

- Management.

- Email marketing.

- Social media marketing.

- Search engine optimization (SEO).

- Writing.

If you already have a blog, you might have some of these skills. If you can acquire any new skills that you don't currently have, and successfully implement them, then you can learn to be a professional blogger.

You have to be different from every blogger out there. You have to be unique. You have to be special. You have to be better than everybody else in your field.

To be able to do this, you have to strengthen your weaknesses:

- If you can't figure out what is wrong, ask for feedback.

- If your blog is boring, find ways to engage with others more.

- If your writing isn't that great, practice your writing.

1. Figure Out What You Want

If you want peace of mind when you are transitioning into professional blogging, the first thing you need to do is to figure out ways to make a recurring fixed income with your blog. When you are positive that you can survive comfortably from your blog, only then should you even think about quitting your job to be a full-time blogger.

Before you take this important step, make sure to write out a business plan and road map. You need to think about these things:

- Are you willing to learn new things?

- Are there ways to expand your blog?

- Are there ways you can bring attention to your blog?

- How will you brand your blog?

- What sources of income are you going to use?

- What will your marketing strategy look like?

- Where will you get your traffic?

You have to take the time to think about and develop your blog. What do you want it to be like? This is a very important stage for you, to grow your blog and for you to identify avenues to develop it in the future.

2. Being a Professional Blogger

It could take you anywhere from six months to a number of years to make the decision to become a professional blogger. The blogging world has gotten larger over the past few years. You need to be well equipped to rely on blogging as your full-time income.

Keep in mind the old quote: "Never put all your eggs in one basket."

Even though the blogging world is volatile, when you are trying to become a professional blogger, you have to protect yourself in every way possible. If you only have one blog that is making you money, you need to try to expand your empire so that a catastrophic problem doesn't bankrupt you.

If you have a good blog, you might begin making a decent amount of money in about four to five months.

3. College Students

If you are a college student, you need to start a blog. Being in college allows you to have many social engagements, freedom, and endless opportunities to get your life ready for success. If you can publish a blog with ten articles each month, by the end of your first year you will have published 120 articles. By the time you graduate from college, you will have a well-aged blog with about 500 articles.

Passive Income: Your Game Changer

Let's begin by finding out what passive income actually is: passive income is money that you earn in ways that don't take a lot of effort. Some types of passive income include renting out property that you own, or blogging. It might take some time and effort to get these revenue streams started, but then you can make money while you are sleeping.

To many people, blogging is just a hobby. If you want to make lots of money, you need to look at it as a business. Some bloggers are going to struggle to make enough money to cover the expenses of running their blog, like their electric and internet bills. Other bloggers have pulled in over one million dollars each year. While nothing is ever guaranteed, I can tell you that if you are diligent, your rewards could be tremendous.

How much money you make all depends on the traffic your site gets. You can make between one and ten cents per page view. This means that if you generate about 50,000 views each month, you will be making between $500 and $5,000 each month.

There aren't any definitive sources on the amount of money you could make blogging, but one survey done by a website called ProBlogger surveyed 1,500 bloggers and found the following:

- Four percent brought in a five-figure salary each month.

- Thirteen percent made above $1,000 each month.

- Fifty-three percent made less than $100 each month.

- Ten percent didn't make anything.

4. How to Make Money

You can make money with your blog and with opportunities that might show up because you have a site. Here are some methods:

1. Services.

Blogging creates credibility and could help make you seem like an expert on a certain subject. This will give you an opportunity to maneuver into services that pay, like:

- Investments.

- Performing specific services like social media marketing, fixing websites, or creating websites.

- Speaking.

- Coaching.

2. Selling products.

To do this you just have to use your blog's content to make readers want to purchase a product from your site. These can be separated into digital and physical products:

- Digital.

- Memberships.

- Exclusive access through your site.

- Premium content.

- Online courses.

- E-books.

- Physical.

- Retail items like jewelry, clothing, etc.

- Books.

5. Affiliate marketing.

With this type of marketing, you are going to recommend services or products on your website. You, in turn, will make a commission or percentage of all sales. Companies know you have readers that are loyal and trust you. They will check out other businesses because you recommended them. This doesn't cost your readers anything.

This is a money-making strategy that is powerful for blogs that have a certain niche. If you write about photography and you think that a certain course might be a good fit for your audience, you put a link to this course on your blog and for every signup that happens by clicking on this link, you will get a commission. You could also recommend a product they can purchase from Amazon, then you get paid if somebody purchases something through your site.

You can create your relationships with companies that work with your niche or you can use a company such as Flex Offers or Commission Junction.

Affiliate marketing has the potential to be a great deal for everybody, since businesses are getting introduced to audiences, readers are finding out about services or products, and you get a commission from connecting the two.

6. Advertising.

Advertisers are looking for ways to get exposed and to find new customers. If you give them a place to be seen, you could get money for it. This type of advertising comes in many forms:

- Sponsored Posts: This is a type of marketing that involves creating and sharing material like social media posts, blogs, and videos that don't promote a brand but want to create an interest in its services or products. Businesses want their products to be seen on various sites and know that through links it will help their ratings. They are usually willing to pay you between $50 and thousands of dollars to put their products or services on your blog.

- Brand Partnerships: Companies are willing to pay influencers. Blogging can be a great way to capitalize on this, but people who use Instagram usually do particularly well with it. Companies know that certain people have audiences that can be reached through association with them. All they want you to do is to refer, wear, or mention them on your blog or Instagram account.

- Display Advertising: You may have been on a site where you saw an ad on a sidebar or in the upper banner spot. You might see some in email posts or in newsletters.

- Contextual Ads: You will use a company such as Mediavine, Media.net, or Google AdSense. You are giving a space on your blog to a company that will fill that space with ads that your audience will see. You might have noticed that what you search for on Google follows you onto specific sites, where your searches suddenly show up as ads. This is a contextual ad. You could get paid for how many times the ad is clicked on or seen by visitors to your site. This is called either cost per click or cost per impression.

• Private/Direct Ads: You will work with the company to display their product. This is also called a banner or static ad. The company will choose what they would like to show in a specific size box on your blog. You will set a price and they will pay you yearly, monthly, or daily to keep this on your blog.

7. Making It Successful

This part isn't all that easy. Anyone who has ever told you that you can just "Put some content up and begin bringing in the cash" is lying. It is going to take time to understand that running a blog is like running a business. You have to create your content and then build up trust and readers. Here are some steps you need to take:

• Create Your Blog: There have been many people who say they want to make money with their blog but they don't ever do this step. You need to begin somewhere.

• Find Content: You have to create content that will focus on specific niches that you are passionate about and that will draw in readers. You want a niche that is big enough for an audience but not so huge that you are going to get lost in the crowd.

• You Have to Stay Consistent: You have to be sure you are creating content consistently. This will help build a brand and people will want to see your content.

• Promoting Your Blog: It is wonderful for you to write an amazing blog, but what happens if nobody knows about it? You have to be active on social media. You have to network with other bloggers. Never be afraid of letting people know you are out there.

8. Will It Be Worth It?

This all depends on what you want out of it. You might not have any expectations as to the amount of money you can make blogging. I know I began my blog as a dare but it has turned into a lot more.

Most blogs will die before they are one year old. This is because, at first, you spend a lot of time writing without getting any money from it. It doesn't make sense when you look at it on paper, but if you can learn to be persistent, all the hard work will pay off with time. This sounds very much like passive income. You work hard at first then you get the payoff later.

You have to build a relationship with your readers, too. You can't measure that in money, but these readers are valuable in other ways.

Beginning a blog will allow you to be more flexible if you have a day job that you absolutely love and don't want to give up. You will be able to switch shifts, give up a shift or two, spend time with friends and family, and have more freedom overall.

If this sounds good to you, beginning a blog might be worth the time and effort.

$10,000+ a Month: Success Stories of Popular Bloggers

Blogging can be very profitable. I am sure you are wondering how in the world these bloggers can bring in loads of profits. Well, I have found the most successful bloggers who were willing to tell me their success stories and give us a sneak peek at what they do behind the scenes.

9. Neil Patel

Neil is an internet marketing guru who has earned over one million dollars a year with blogging. He is also a digital marketer who runs Hello Bar, QuickSprout, and Kissmetrics. He credits blogging with being his best revenue generator. He puts aside between five and six thousand dollars to help with his blog creations. He brings in over seven hundred thousand visitors in just one month. This turns into over 8,000 leads. These leads came solely from his blog. Here are some pointers from Neil:

- Your page subheadings and title only give you a few seconds to grab a person's attention. These sections count tremendously. You have to show your readers in the blink of an eye what they can expect when they read your blog.

- The length of your article doesn't matter as long as the point is clear and valuable. Don't forget the visual aids.

- Your blog needs to give your readers advice that is valuable, actionable, and clear.

- Network with other bloggers. Make sure you answer everybody's questions in a timely manner and make them actionable, helpful and detailed. Don't give them fluff.

- Add in an "opt-in" box at the end of all your blogs.

- Your content has to be exceptional to increase the traffic to your blog.

10. Pat Flynn

He has earned over two hundred thousand dollars in just one year. He went from being unemployed to being an internet sensation in a very short time. His blog called Smart Passive Income has made about two million dollars in revenue. Here are some of the things he did to accomplish this:

- Be a consultant. These services are something that can't be outsourced and are a great source of income. You have to create a good reputation and have quality learning materials so you can make your price large enough to be worthwhile.

- Online courses. Selling courses online is great since you only have to spend some money and time to make these. From there, you just resell them as long as they don't become obsolete.

- Create a podcast. Some people are visual learners, while others are auditory. Some people might just be too busy to read. Podcasts allow you to serve various audiences. If you do decide to create a podcast, add in a transcript.

- Make a membership site. This is a great source of stable and recurring income. Make sure your members get quality support and content.

- Write an e-book and publish it. Write about something you know well. You could also compile all your blogs into one book and sell these, too.

- Write about what you know and love. You can educate your readers with your blog posts.

11. Matthew Woodward

He is an internet marketing blogger who brings in over $20,000 each month. His success proves that anybody can make a living with blogging. He didn't use any links or SEO strategies. His entire blog is a case study about what happens if you only followed Google's Webmaster Guidelines without any SEO.

As of November 2017, he has earned well over one million dollars. His monthly revenue averages about $20,000. He earns his money from consultations, ads, and affiliate commissions. Here are some pointers from Matthew:

- Create competitions.

- Create video tutorials. Remember to post the transcript.

- Offer your readers exclusive content if they share or sign up. Be sure you offer them something they can't resist.

- When you set up your blog, you need to have an end goal in mind. It might be making money through affiliate commissions, selling products, subscribing to emails, social media, or a newsletter.

- You have to write the way you speak. You need to be straightforward and direct.

- Create a section of your blog for questions. This can be your topic for the next blog.

- Post your blog on forums like WarriorForum and TrafficPlanet. Interact with readers through their comments and always reply to their emails.

- Know what your audience wants and create your content from there.

12. Ramit Sethi

He created the I Will Teach You To Be Rich Blog. He earned five million dollars in just six days. He has over one million readers each month and has eight hundred thousand subscribers to his newsletter. Here is some advice he freely gives:

- Take an hour daily for some strategizing.

- Don't work with cheap clicks – they won't give you much revenue. Use quality products or services, deliver, and charge.

- If you have a customer who is interested in your product but you know it won't work for them, tell them and point them toward another product that will. Yes, you will be losing a sale but you will be gaining a person's trust.

- Whatever content you choose to write about, make sure 80 percent is valuable and leave the other 20 percent for your sales pitches.

- Know exactly what you want your ideal customer to be. Visualize your business as a high-end boutique where you only serve the best work, you can choose who you allow inside.

- Give away free material. After you have established that you are a quality provider, you can start charging big bucks for the products you sell.

- Don't spread yourself too thin. Focus on just a few great things at a time.

- If you don't want to be another fly by night business, don't conform to the standard. Follow your taste and find your vibe. People will soon be flocking to your products. Just don't try to reinvent the wheel with everything.

- Focus on finding 1,000 loyal customers who will stand by you and your products. This is better than having hundreds of thousands of readers who aren't interested at all.

13. Lena Gott

She is the founder and blogger of What Mommy Does. She earns more than $10,000 each month. Since she is a stay at home mom, she works anywhere between 20 and 25 hours weekly, which is hard to do with children. She makes her money from affiliate commissions, sponsored posts, e-books, and ads. Here are some pointers from her:

- Be useful and helpful. This is the best way to get your readers' trust.

- Add in other media. You don't have to pen a novel.

- One post should equal a solution. Remain focused on one idea and don't stray from it. The more specific, the better.

- Get to know your readers better and figure out what problems they might need help with.

- Make sure your ideas are validated before you spend money on ads. It is best to test ideas on a small scale and then add in paid ads later, instead of spending money not knowing if it will pay off in the long run.

- Find what content brings you the most profit. Focus on getting more page views to those articles and create more like these. Your goal shouldn't be on page views but on page views to the pages that bring in the profits.

14. Robbie Richards

His blog earnings are over $5,000 each month. He brings in this money through affiliate revenue and he doesn't spend one penny on ads or other traffic strategies. He has been able to boost his traffic by 402 percent, monetize his email list, get over 4,000 subscribers, and increase email sign-ups seven times. Here are some tips from Robbie:

- Utilize smart links to change the opt-in forms that you show to a new reader and an existing subscriber. This allows you to show new readers an opt-in subscription form while showing an existing customer an app coupon, webinar, or new e-book link.

- Use a lead magnet for pages that get a lot of traffic. This lets you put all your best offers on one page.

- Use Thrive Content Builder to change up your landing page by using the "Upside Down Homepage" technique. This will put your opt-in form at the top of the page in banner form, where it will get the best attention.

- Change the subject heading on your emails and then resend the newsletter to anyone who didn't open it the first time.

- Place your post near the top of your Twitter page. Use an automatic scheduler and set it to post on your social media platforms multiple times during a month. Change up your hashtags and taglines.

• When you relaunch any updated content, change the published date, too. Reach out to people who commented, shared, or promoted the article before. Tell them about the update.

• Use subheadings and headlines that are catchy and state the benefits that the reader will get.

• If your posts are long, reformat them into articles that are more readable. Break up long paragraphs into three-or-four-sentence snippets. Add in media or images per 100 words and have a clickable table of contents.

• Re-publish, update, and optimize posts that already exist that correspond to your keywords.

• Use sorting techniques, conditional formatting, and filters to help you sift through keywords.

• Do a keyword search for existing content and find which ones show up more. Any words that rank between six and twenty and have an average of 300 hits per month are what you want to choose.

Aim Higher: Setting New Goals

Being human, we are bad at thinking about compound growth. We like to think linearly. We like overestimating the things we can achieve in a short amount of time but we underestimate the long run. Setting the right goals lets you tie your big ambitions with your daily tactics so you won't get in too deep but it won't let you sell yourself short, either.

Let's look at some methods you can do now to take your blog to the next level. We will look at the main components of goals that are workable, and how to form and develop them. I'll also show you how to implement these strategies, putting them into practice, sticking with them, keeping track of your achievements, and some roadblocks you might encounter.

15. Begin with "Why?"

The main question you have to ask yourself is: "Why did I create this blog?" What do you want to achieve by running it?

If you blindly pick and choose a goal, it will make it harder for you to find the drive to achieve it. Take some time and write down some outlines or ideas that you think should be the purpose of your blog. Then figure out where you want to take your business.

16. SMART Goals

Once you have the wherefores and whys out of the way, let's figure out how to set effective and manageable goals. These will make sure that you are targeting improvable, specific areas and you are setting yourself up for long-term, sustainable growth.

The SMART system has been used by many to set goals. You might have heard about it, but let's look at it in depth. SMART is a checklist that makes sure you are able to attain your goals in the best way possible. SMART stands for:

> • **Specific**: You have to narrow down your plans to specific goals. If you don't, you won't know whether or not you are succeeding.
>
> • **Measurable**: You have to be able to measure your goals so they can be effective. "Being a better writer" can't be measured, but "Writing a post that gets one hundred shares" can be measured.
>
> • **Achievable**: You might eventually get 10,000 people to read your blog. But you can't expect this in the first month. You have to begin small and work your way up. Focus on what is possible or you are going to be very disappointed.

- **Relevant**: You have to make sure your goals are relevant to why you are creating a blog.

- **Time-bound**: The best way to ignore anything is not to put any time constraints on it. Having the goal of "writing ten blogs" has a different urgency than "writing ten blogs by November." When you put hard limits on your time, you will make sure that you have a purpose to do things now.

What do **SMART** goals look like when blogging? Let's split them into three types of goals:

- **Optimization goals**: these will relate to how you understand the process of making goals:

    - "Set up Google Analytics for the blog and check these numbers weekly and update the results on a spreadsheet."

    - "Read and take notes on four main articles during the next two weeks."

- **Performance goals**: these will relate to how your blog is doing:

    - "Increase email sign-up rates by twenty percent in the next three months."

    - "Publish more blogs this quarter than last quarter."

    - "Increase traffic by ten percent in one month."

- **Creation goals**: these will be about creating targets for your output:

    - "Publish to a new market, like a podcast or a video, to reach new audiences."

    - "Create three new blog concepts."

- "Write five hundred words every day for one week."

Look back on the list you created earlier. You should be getting a sense of how you can take those ideas and turn them into SMART goals. As a starting point: take those ideas and develop five concrete goals from them.

17. Following Through

By now you should have a notion about the type of format you need to use for your goals to make them effective. What can you use to achieve your goals? Let's look at some obvious points first:

- Never create too many goals. It would be better to reach a few goals than to fail at ten. Build on your successes and make it a priority to use what works for you, instead of trying to succeed at all things.

- Write down your goals and place them where you will see them every day, so you are motivated to reach them.

- Figure out what you aren't going to prioritize. Create clear boundaries between what you are and aren't going to worry about when you are working toward a certain goal. When you can set boundaries, you are removing any interference that might cause you to feel like you are failing.

- Create goal triggers. Instead of telling yourself to write each week, try to set a goal of writing on Tuesday after you eat lunch. This goes back to the "time-bound" section of your SMART goals. This can help you establish concrete and routine times to work on your goals.

18. Review Process

You will choose and then keep track of the most important goals, whether they are quarterly, weekly, or daily. This will make it easier to set smaller goals and lets you work more effectively on small tasks.

The biggest benefit of this is avoiding traps to respond to what is urgent rather than what is important. This helps you prioritize your blog content. Most of these things are completely unrealistic with the amount of time they demand of you. So how does this review process work?

- For example, when you are working on quarterly goals, you need to work on three blogs for the next thirteen weeks. Look back at your last quarter: your failures, achievements, and accomplishments. Do you need to adjust any goals? Now, create goals for the next quarter and narrow them down.

- Setting weekly goals is very similar. You just break your quarterly goals down into shorter time frames – for example, weeks one through five, or six through ten. This should only take you a few minutes.

- You shouldn't have to set any daily goals, but use these same principles when you are working throughout the week. Create three "to-dos" when you are working on your blog, and base them on your weekly goals. This is an effective way to make you focus on what is important.

19. Track Your Achievements

It is very important that you keep track of your goals and achievements. Humans don't do well at keeping a lot of different thoughts in mind at one time. This is why we write things down. Make sure you have your goals written down, to keep you organized and motivated. It is very satisfying to look back at your goals and seeing everything that you have achieved.

Keeping track of your achievements is just one way to keep yourself accountable. There are many ways to keep track of these; you just have to figure out what works best for you. The best way to make sure you stick with your goals is by external accountability. There are many ways you can do this:

- Be accountable to a lot of people by posting updates on social media about your progress toward your goals.

- Up your personal stakes by using a service like stickK or Beeminder. These use a "nudge" theory to motivate you to stick to your goals.

- Talk about your goals with friends or family at least once a week.

- This part of reaching your goals is easy to skip because it takes time. Since you are working on your blog instead of "in" your blog, it is important when trying to make progress.

20. Common Roadblocks

Most people don't make goals because most of the time life happens and we don't reach them. You have read this book this far, so you are trying to improve your life and learn new things. You have already overcome one hurdle: you haven't given up.

Just because you set a goal once and it didn't happen, doesn't mean you won't ever reach a goal. Here are three common roadblocks that most people encounter when they set goals, and how to stay away from them:

- Setting too many goals at one time. If you think about it, you could set 100 goals to help you improve. But if you try to do them all at one time, you are going to get overwhelmed and find that you can't achieve even one of them. Three is the best number.

- Setting goals that aren't focused on. It is great to begin blogging – but what does it really mean? Do you want to strike up a lovely discussion on a specific topic? Do you want your thoughts and ideas to be expressed by talking or writing about them on various sites? Would you like to be a guest writer on other sites? Why do you want to do these things? You have to focus.

• Setting goals that are unrealistic. If you tell yourself that you will reach 10,000 views in one month, this isn't achievable if you aren't already a well-known writer. You can't beat yourself up just because you are getting only 100 views each month when other blogs are pulling in a lot more.

What you have learned by now should help you figure out what is wrong, and ways to solve these problems. The main thing you have to do is set a few, achievable, focused goals, and then stick with them. If this sounds a lot like common sense, it is. We have been told to "dream big" and that is usually our first impulse.

The main thing is to not ever give up. You need to focus on slow growth that will compound. Tie these to other goals and you will begin to see results.

Chapter 2: Blogging Secret #1: Content Marketing

Now that you have decided to start a blog, it is a good time to think about what the future might hold for bloggers and the content marketing world. Upcoming trends indicate that blogs are going to continue being popular, but the content that is created and the way people produce blogs will constantly evolve.

In this chapter, we will be covering the most profitable niches, the dos and don'ts of blogging, hacks, tricks, and content tips, email marketing made simple, and proven strategies.

Niche is King: Profitable Niches Revealed

Blogging is the main type of content marketing and each is very integrated. A great blog will focus on three metrics: good design, regular publishing, and quality content. Editing support and collaboration is just as important as using media such as audios, videos, and images. Research and updates could help build your authority and leadership about your chosen blog content. If you want to use content marketing strategy as a way to make money with your blog, you need to learn the trends, facts, and statistics.

The best niches are the ones that offer profitability, demand, and fulfillment. You could think about niches as what to major in when going to college. Courses like computer engineering and finance make sense if your priority is to earn a large salary. Teaching or being a social worker could be fulfilling but they come with a lower salary. Neither one of these options is wrong or right. What is important is you have to know what you want. After that, you can pick a niche that will be in alignment with your goals.

You can't become a teacher if your main priority is to bring in a six-figure income straight out of college. If you want to make money with your blog, you can't pick a niche that is hard to make money from. This sounds obvious, but it is a very common mistake that many people make.

It doesn't matter if you have been blogging for a long time or are new to the blogging business, what is important is to give serious thought to which niche to choose. Let's look at the three main factors when picking a niche:

- **Profitability**

- The best blog ideas are ones where you offer great value to others by helping a lot of people solve their problems. Now, you need to figure out if your idea will be profitable. This is very easy.

- You just have to ask yourself this question: "Do other bloggers make money in this niche?"

Competition is a good thing in the blogging world. There will probably be many blogs on whatever niche you decide to enter into. It is easier to make money in larger niches, since companies have realized how powerful blogs have become as a marketing tool.

There are many opportunities to make money with:

- Advertising.

- Sponsored content.

- Affiliate marketing.

The main questions you need to ask when picking your niche are:

- Do bloggers make money in this niche?

- What could I make that can offer the best value to others?

•Demand

Creating value is about helping others. What you make that gives the best value to a large number of people will maximize demand. A common trait that many blogs share is they help solve problems. This does sound simple. Solving problems is creating value. When you can help others solve their problems, you will have a better chance of success.

•Fulfillment

Everyone is familiar with the saying: "Follow your passion and success will follow." This advice is always given freely but it could be quite dangerous if you follow it. Your passion will come after you have worked hard to get excellent at something that is valuable. So, basically, what you do is not as important as how you do it.

If you ever want to love what you do, you have to get rid of the mindset of: "What can the world offer me?" You need to think: "What can I give to the world?"

Let's begin here: "What can I make that will give the largest value to the world?"

This mindset will put you on the path to fulfillment and it will give you the biggest chance for success. You have to find things that you are passionate about so you can find the niche where you can give the most.

If you have a lot of experience in a certain field, this is where you can provide the largest value. Expertise and experience aren't required. If you just have something that you are passionate about or something you are going through that you think will resonate with readers, write about that. Your blog can be about when you solved a huge problem, or just sharing your journey.

Most Popular Niche Ideas

My goal here is to help you find better ways to save and make money. Let's look at the most profitable, proven blog niches along with the cons and pros of each. All of these have already passed the test and they will make you money. You will need to narrow the choices down within each niche.

1. Travel.

In order to have a great travel blog, you need to:

- •Know how to get traffic from SEOs and social media.

- •Inspire others to get out and enjoy life.

- •Have a certain audience to build content for.

Basically, none of these points should be surprising to you. Creating content, SEO, and social media around a certain demographic is what makes blogs successful.

Cons:

- Larger up-front costs for travel.

- There isn't a large opportunity to sell expensive products to this kind of audience since people's budgets usually go to their travel expenses.

- Most blog content revolves around traveling, so you need to be able and willing to do a lot of traveling now and in the future.

Pros:

- It is fun.

- Great potential to make money by referring credit cards.

- Create content that is linked to niches that are related to travel hacking and making money when traveling.

2. Multi-Niche or Lifestyle.

It is easy to create a blog that is based on a niche. The main trend you can't ignore is the dozens of multi-niche blogs that have been successful and are taking the blogging world by storm. These bloggers create a content strategy about what interests them.

If you take a deep dive into successful multi-niche blogs, you will see that their content is extremely calculated and usually focuses on creating content that can drive traffic through Pinterest.

Successful multi-niche blogs will focus on solving issues around a certain demographic. A millennial lifestyle blog might focus on relationships, career, travel, and finance. Mommy blogs might focus on cooking, cleaning, home life, and parenting.

Cons:

- Your audience might have a different problem that your blog doesn't cover and this makes it harder to come up with a content strategy.

- It might be hard to rank on Google if your content is broad instead of more deeply focused on one topic.

Pros:

- More money-making opportunities.

- Keep things interesting if you get bored with certain topics.

- You can switch up topics based on new trends.

3. Fitness and Health.

The biggest benefit of the fitness and health niche is that these readers are hungry for information. People are looking for answers to their questions and they want them "yesterday." It would be great to use Pinterest for this niche. It will be easy to build a lot of traffic to your blog. Many fitness and health blogs make money by using affiliate programs. The bloggers who make the big bucks have products that will solve their audience's problems.

Cons:

> • Seasonal – usually peaks around January.
>
> • This topic is very competitive.

Pros:

> • Makes money in various ways: from expensive products to affiliate revenue.

4. Investing and Personal Finance.

This is my favorite niche of all. There is a huge demand on Pinterest for topics that deal with saving money and living a frugal life. Because of this, you could build traffic fairly fast while creating an SEO strategy at the same time. The biggest money-making blogs focus on making money (shocker) because this is obviously what people want to know.

Cons:

> • It is a competitive space within search engines and most large publishing companies will fight over this traffic.
>
> • It can be seasonal. Interest usually peaks between November and February.

Pros:

> • Information on how to manage finances and make smart investments is in high demand.
>
> • Can turn into a money-making niche when you have a large following.

5. Fashion.

This niche is extremely visual. This is good, since social media is becoming more visual, with highly successful sites like YouTube, Pinterest, and Instagram. Affiliate marketing, sponsored content, and display ads are the most common money-making strategies.

Cons:

- Not great for trying to sell expensive products.

- Your brand is visually based around you.

Pros:

- Many opportunities on less competitive and visual networks like YouTube, Pinterest, and Instagram.

- It is possible to make money with affiliate programs selling accessories and clothing.

6. Food.

Food bloggers make money through advertising. This means you have to generate many page views before you will be successful with your blog. You can do this fairly fast by having a good strategy using Pinterest. There is a lot of competition in culinary areas like vegan, keto, and paleo. If you are interested in this niche, do tons of research beforehand, using "Google Trends." Try to find a trend that is just beginning to gain some traction. It would have been a great time to begin a blog focusing on paleo during 2009.

Cons:

- Most people want to find free recipes, so you normally can't sell products.

- It is a labor of love to create new recipes. You have to test them, take pictures, and write all the content.

Pros:

- New trends usually emerge extremely fast and this can create great opportunities if you can react fast enough.

- There are many brands in this space and this lets you use sponsored posts.

- This topic is in high demand for both social media and search engines.

7. Crafts and DIY.

The largest niches on Pinterest are do-it-yourself (DIY), crafts, arts, and sewing. Because it is easier to get traffic to new sites via Pinterest, compared to Google, you could build a very successful blog extremely fast.

Cons:

- Hard to sell expensive products.

Pros:

- A wonderful visual niche that has huge potential on YouTube.

- Can sell products on Etsy or Shopify.

- Huge potential on social media and search engines: especially Pinterest.

8. Marketing and Business.

An old proverb says: "In the land of the blind, the one-eyed man is king."

This is basically saying that if you compare yourself to others who have no skills in a certain area, even having a small level of skill puts you in a stronger position than the competition. This is an important concept to remember when you want to get into the most competitive niche: marketing and business.

If you want to begin a blog that deals with making money, you are going to be competing with the smartest bloggers in the world. But let's say, for example, you actually begin a blog about marketing specifically for freight brokers – a niche industry that finds carriers to ship freight. Here, you are the one-eyed man in a room full of blind people. This is what you want to be, metaphorically speaking, and where you will most likely find success as a blogger in the competitive scene of marketing and business blogging.

Cons:

- This is a field that is crowded and you will be competing with some bloggers who have more experience.

Pros:

- You will sharpen your marketing and business skills.

- You can sell expensive products along with consulting services.

Bottom Line

If you are thinking about beginning a blog and you know you have a great niche in mind, the only thing I can say is to do it. You aren't going to know everything about the topic today, but when it comes to blogging, you actually learn on the job.

Mastering Blog Posts: The Dos and Don'ts

Would you like to know how to write a blog post that will convert? Do your posts convert the way you want them to? We are going to cover some tips that will help you write blogs that will convert.

You might see that many people who visit your blog usually leave without reading it completely. What's worse is that more people who see your post on social media, like Facebook and Twitter, won't even click on it.

You only have about two to three seconds to grab a person's attention and convince them to click on and read your post. How can you make sure your marketing efforts aren't being wasted? If you follow these tips, you will soon be writing posts that will convert.

- **Call-to-action**

You have to add a clear call-to-action. It doesn't matter if you ask your readers to purchase something, follow you on your social media accounts, share your post, or leave a comment, just be sure you state what you want them to do clearly.

This needs to be something that stands out and is easily distinguishable. You could say something like: "If you like this post, then I'd like it if you would share this on Facebook and Twitter."

- **Optimize SEO**

I don't recommend that you write for SEO, but it doesn't hurt to keep SEO in mind while you write. Google searches drive a large amount of traffic for many websites. If you want to maximize your ranking on Google, you need to optimize your posts for the most important ranking factors.

Here are some tips to keep in mind:

- Interlink content.
- Add images.
- Use variations of keywords.
- Optimize the focus keyword.
- Add in the right meta description.
- Add in the right meta title.
- **Images**

The human brain will process visual content faster than just words. This is why you need to add images that captivate audiences and that will help engage others. There are many free resources that offer free images.

• Bullet Points

Everybody will skim down a page before they read it, so you need to highlight your most important information. Bullet points are great, since they are easy to see and skim. Here are tips to use when writing bullet points that people will stop to read:

- Express your clear intent. Bullet points are miniature headlines.

- Don't clutter your bullet points. Don't write paragraphs.

- Keep the bullet points symmetrical. Try for no more than two lines.

• Subheadings

Getting your formatting correct is critical for blogs. There isn't anything worse than reading a blog that is one huge paragraph. Most people will just skim through before they read the whole post. It is recommended that you break up the article by using subheadings. Whatever you can do to make it easier for the user to read your blog, so they will take any actions you might want them to do.

• Headlines

If your headlines aren't compelling, there will be a good chance that your post won't be shared; much less read. Humans are shallow people. We are constantly judging books by their covers and blogs by their titles. This is why it is critical for your blog title to be compelling, or your blog won't be successful. You could use a headline analyzer to find how valuable your headline will be. This can also give you tips on ways to improve the headline.

• Know Your Target Audience

Before you even begin writing, you have to know who your audience is going to be and the things they want. Rather than guessing what your audience wants or needs, do some competitor analysis and industry research. It sounds complicated, doesn't it? Good news, it isn't.

There are many resources you can use and here are some I use frequently:

- SEMRush: this one you have to pay for but it works great and lets you spy on your competitors so you can steal their ideas.

- Quora: This is a great resource to find questions that people are asking within your niche.

- Twitter Advanced Search: all you have to do is type a keyword and then select a filter question. It will then show you any and all questions that people are asking in your niche.

- KeywordTool.io: this is a free tool that lets you see the most popular keywords that people are using in your niche.

I hope these tips are helpful to you. If you can follow these, you will be writing blog posts that successfully convert.

Content Tips, Tricks, and Hacks

Content marketing is a powerful tool that creates serious results. It's a great way to build trust, generate leads, and increase your sales. It's a strategy that any business or anyone who is on a budget can use and benefit from. You might be sitting there thinking: "Been there, done that, it isn't for me." You might just be exploring the idea of content marketing and aren't sure where you should start. It doesn't matter. I can personally tell you that it will work to grow your business and it doesn't have to be complicated. All you need to know is where you have to focus your efforts.

Content marketing is a tool that requires patience, effort, and depending on your preference, it might take some budget or time. Even though it might take some work, many businesses both large and small continue to prioritize content marketing above most other business strategies.

The reason they do this is that they have figured out how to achieve huge results with a very minimal investment. The best way to make content marketing work for you is to be focused on what brings in results, so you don't waste time on things that don't work. It sounds simple, but you have to pay attention to the details.

Here are some tips that have been proven to help you transform your content into the ultimate marketing tool:

- **Start with the End**

The best way to create a plan is to work backward. Before you begin any type of content, you have to be completely clear on what your marketing goals are, and what you want to accomplish. This will shape and streamline your message. This gives each piece of content a purpose.

If you want to generate leads, you will need to brainstorm on content that gives quick wins and will entice visitors to give you their email address. If your goal is increasing sales and you are working farther down the funnel, you may want to think about having a webinar that will showcase your services and products. This creates brand awareness. Then you can check out being a guest on a podcast or hosting your own. Every piece of content will bring prospects closer to being a loyal customer.

- **Know Your Customer**

It will be useless if you create content that your target audience doesn't care about. This totally defeats the purpose of content marketing. All of your content needs to hinge on understanding and knowing your audience. Visualizing your ideal customer avatar is a great way to know that you are creating the perfect content. This perfect avatar needs to include information such as interests, geographic location, profession, and age, so you can get a sense of the type of topics and problems that impact your ideal readers' lives the most. You can leverage this material to make your connection with your audience deeper, by using content that resonates with them. When they feel like you understand them, they will begin to trust and like you. You will need to keep this avatar handy for the next tip, too.

• Salt in Their Wounds

Nothing makes a person want to act more than pain. It doesn't matter if the pain is physical, emotional, or financial. When somebody is hurting, they will be in the market for something that will make the pain go away. You want to stay away from using dramatic or cruel tactics here, but the point is to bring awareness to the discomfort and follow it up by offering a solution.

Look at your customer avatar and see if you can identify their largest "pain points." Use contrast to create a picture that is specific to what life might be like on the other side of their troubles, then offer your services and products as the vehicle to get them there. Could you free up some time so they can eat dinner with their family? Will you give them the confidence they need to approach their boss about a raise that was promised? How could you make their life more productive, brighter, or happier? Use your content to solve their problems.

• Respect the Platform

Your content needs to look like it belongs, and not seem out of place. This means that you have to respect whatever platform you are using, and study what form and style of content works best there. The best way to do this is to look at what other successful bloggers are doing on their platform and then see how you could adapt, customize, and unleash your own version. Also, don't ever be afraid to look outside your niche to get some inspiration.

• Go to Them

Many valuable resources go into making and distributing your content. If it attracts little or no response, it feels like you have wasted money, energy, and time. It will discourage you from moving forward, so you need to do everything in your power to make sure your content doesn't fall on deaf ears, by picking channels and platforms that your market actually uses. This might sound like common sense, but it is easy to get sucked into using a million different social media sites, just because they seem popular today. Do some research and figure out where your market hangs out online. By putting your content on platforms your target audience uses and prefers, you will improve your chances of reaching them and you will stay away from hitting dead ends with your content.

• Share and Syndicate

After you have created some content, don't be afraid to carve it up and share it on other platforms and channels. For example, a video could be turned into a podcast episode, which could be transcribed into a blog post. You could even carve it up more into tweets, Facebook posts, or condensed into articles for LinkedIn. Syndicating your content across other channels is a great way to extend your reach to potential customers who wouldn't have heard of you. For example, somebody who listens to podcasts might spend less time reading blogs. A daily Facebook user might never have a reason to go on LinkedIn. Using some minor tweaks to optimize and freshen up your content for various platforms will stretch your money and reach.

• Call-to-Action

You have just given your audience a huge dose of quality content. Now you need to take the opportunity to help point your prospects in the right direction. So, provide them with the next piece of the puzzle. You can do this by ending each piece of content with a friendly call to action like this: "If you want to discover how to easily turn your marketing strategy into high converting and profitable content, without spending hours stuck at your desk staring at the blank screen of death wondering what to write, then I highly encourage you to download your FREE copy of [whatever you have to offer your customers]."

With all the marketing options out there, content marketing can deliver higher quality leads and customers than just about any other strategy out there. In fact, the marketing institute says that businesses that use content marketing have six times more conversions than businesses that don't. So, get started today by working on applying these tips to make your content marketing more efficient and effective. By doing this, you can provide top-notch value to your customers, increase your impact, and watch your business grow.

Email Marketing Made Simple

You have written an awesome blog post. You have published it but to your horror, no one has read it. Why? Did you promote it with email? If not, why didn't you?

Email marketing is the most effective method of communicating directly with your readers. Encourage people to sign up to your email list with opt-in pop-ups, RSS feeds, and social contests. Then create and send emails to drive a ton of traffic to your blog.

Here are some tips that will help you drive traffic to your blog:

- **Visual Newsletters**

Most people like visual information. You can entice your readers to click on your blog with newsletters full of images. Add-in summaries of articles that let the audience know your main points but end each one with a tease and a clickable button that says: "Read more here."

Don't send out too many newsletters. Your readers have lives, too. Monitor the opened and click-through rates from the emailed newsletters, to figure out the best times and frequency to send your newsletters.

- **Scheduling Articles**

Create a scheduling calendar for your articles to be published. This makes it easier for you. You will be able to keep track of when you need more content.

Sending regular articles to people who have signed up for your newsletter will keep them reading your blog. This creates a habit for your readers, deepens their trust in you, and makes you feel more familiar to them, as they get to know when to expect your next article. You need to schedule your articles in advance.

- **Call-to-Action**

You have to be clear in your emails about what you want from your readers. If you want people to click through to your blog, you have to ask them. You will increase your response rates if you do.

You also have to make it easy for them to act on your request. Make sure the link to your blog post is easy to see and is clickable. You can create colored call to action (CTA) buttons that are embedded in your email. You could use a formatting site like MailChimp, Fusion, and Stamplia to make your CTA buttons easier to create. These are highly effective, so don't forget to use them.

- **Segmenting Emails**

You need to segment your email list into more targeted groups, based on what your business needs. Send out your newsletters and blog articles to people who actually read it. You could even create various emails and newsletters and link them to the same article.

If you are sending an email to a business supplier, you want to send them different emails than the ones you are sending to your customers.

- **Personalize Notes**

You need to keep your emails personalized. Include names and other personal details that you know about your email subscribers. If your articles are related to their business, mention the business name, and how your post is going to help them. Personalizing emails will increase the click-through rate by about thirteen percent.

• Get Real

To get people to click through to your blog, make the email content real. Impersonal, corporate, or stock emails aren't going to get any results today. You have to remember that you are competing with thousands of other emails in a person's inbox.

You have to write your emails as if you are sending a message to a friend. Use words like "me" and "you" in the content. Create a tone that will resonate with your demographics. Make sure it is professional but at the same time conversational.

Deepen the relationship with your subscribers by keeping it real and inviting them to join you on your blog.

• Subject Line

The subject line of your email can make or break you before anyone ever reads your message. You have to take the time to create a good subject line. Make sure it is short but to the point and don't forget the "call to action". Convey a great benefit, a state of disbelief, a sense of urgency, or ask questions in your email.

Test your subject lines and find the ones that are getting opened the most, read, and clicked-through, and use this information to improve them in the future.

• Email to Get Emails

You have to use your email to get in touch with many people. Use your signature to get people to click through to your blog. Create a friendly call to action in the email signature and invite contacts to visit your blog. Add in a brief benefit to motivate some action. Tell them what your blog is about. Don't forget to include an easy link to click.

- **Opt-in Pop-ups**

I know that newsletter pop-ups are annoying but they can also work to increase your subscribers. They actually work so well that most bloggers, whether they are single bloggers or corporate bloggers, will use them.

Implement the pop-up efficiently by placing it correctly and by using a pop-up builder. Give reasons for why visitors to your site need to have your newsletter, and how your products or services will make their lives better. Use words like "exclusive content" or "free" and keep the tone friendly, and you will get more people to sign up.

- **Create RSS Feeds**

Make it easy for people to keep in touch with you once they have visited your site. Create and set up an RSS subscription button on your site. Make sure it is a contrasting color and make it visible close to the top of the page.

- **Generating Social Email Tips**

There are many effective and cool ways to get people signing up to your email through social platforms. You could include a link on all your social media platforms that will take people to your blog. You could post content like coupons, e-books, and webinars. You could also make Facebook tabs full of exclusive offers and incentives.

- **Get Leads from Campaigns**

You have probably hosted campaigns like sweepstakes and contests. Most businesses do. Social contests help you spread your brand but they are also a way to get more emails. Have a sweepstake on your blog, Twitter, or Facebook. Ask for people's email as a way for them to enter.

You can also motivate people to spread the word about your offer by doing a referral campaign: this gives them deals for telling their friends to give you their emails.

Proven Strategies: The Blog Niche That Made $100k in 9 Months

Jeff Rose spent nine months constantly blogging before he even made his first $100. That equals about 17 cents an hour. Can you imagine working a full-time job and only making 17 cents an hour? You would have quit on your first day.

Jeff didn't quit, he learned from his mistakes and began a new site, where he made over $100K in only nine months. Let's find out how.

Jeff realized that there were ways to use Google AdSense, banner ads, and affiliate marketing to make money. He decided to see what all the fuss was about, and began networking to find people who could show him how he could make money with his blog

Once Jeff began making money, he got the idea to begin another site. On his new site, he talked about insurance, investing, and financial planning. He figured out that one area he was getting paid a lot through Google ads was with life insurance. Using Google AdWords, Jeff saw which life insurance companies and marketers were willing to pay per click just to have their ads displayed on websites and Google searches. He knew that if insurance companies were willing to pay anywhere between $25 to $50 per click to have their ad displayed on a person's website, they would be willing to pay more per lead. He wondered how much he was missing out on when it came to life insurance commissions, since he was giving it away through Google ads and only getting a pay-per-click.

Since Jeff was a financial planner, he was able to sell life insurance products, such as term life insurance. He decided to try to sell term life insurance policies through his site, rather than just making money with pay-per-click. He started a journey of making phone calls and eventually found an insurance brokerage that focused on online leads. Through talking to them, he found there was tons of revenue out there that he was leaving behind. He was shown other insurance blogs and sites and how well they were doing, including one particular site that was bringing in around $50,000 per month. When Jeff realized that, he said to himself: "I can do that."

Using the website GoDaddy, Jeff registered his new domain name. He had his website, he had the motivation, and he knew he could make money from this site. Now, he had to figure out how to create the content and get people to actually go to his site and then want to give him their email address or call him for a quote.

He did keyword research. He used the tool called SEMRush and he still uses it today. This tool lets you find competitive keywords from various sites that you might be tracking. He checked out his competition to see what kind of content they were producing so he could replicate it on his site.

During the time he was getting his new site running, Jeff was also working as a financial planner, he had his old site that he was still blogging on, and he had a family. He had a lot going on in his life and he didn't have a lot of time to put into this new site. He wanted to make sure he could outsource as much work as he could and still get the best results. So, Jeff decided to use an app called Mobile Assistant where he used his cell phone to transcribe his blog and then it was typed up within 48 hours and emailed back to him. He then put this on his blog. This app does cost money per month but it is worth it.

Jeff also decided to outsource some of his writing. He advises that you do the research and find a site that will give you quality work. Don't just use a company because it is cheap. Use one that will give you the high quality work that you need and want. You will pay more money for quality but if you want a successful company, you are going to have to pay out some money to bring in customers.

Jeff published quality content and promoted that content on all the social media sites. He offered various types of media. He created podcasts and put them on various social media sites that backlinked to his life insurance website.

The best thing you can do to create a great blog is to do a huge amount of research on keywords and be well educated in your chosen niche. You have to network and just work hard. It is important to use social media to feed into your main blog, and the more media you can offer, the better off you will be. You have to be willing to call, email, and keep in touch with people who have visited your site in order to make money.

Chapter 3: Blogging Secret #2: Setting Your Mindset

You can use affiliate marketing to help your blog make money for you. I will teach you the basics of affiliate marketing, along with some strategies, networks, how to use Amazon, etc. Read on to find out everything you need to know about affiliate marketing.

How Affiliate Marketing Can Work for Your Blog

Affiliate marketing is where you get money from promoting somebody else's program, service, or product. You promote whatever it is by providing your readers with a special link on your blog. When they click your link and then buy a product, you will either get a percentage or a specified rate for that sale.

It is a win-win for everyone involved, with these benefits:

- A person who buys the program, service, or product gets exposed to something that is beneficial or helpful that they might not have known about.

- The person or brand that has the program, service, or product will be getting more sales that they might not have gotten on their own, so this is making more money for them and more of an impact on their company. This makes them happy to give away some profits.

• You are sharing helpful resources and information with your readers that will improve their lives, plus you are making money.

You should only promote services or brands that you have tried, trust, and love. The affiliate needs to be in alignment with your personal mission or philosophy.

You may have to turn down some sponsors or affiliates due to questionable business practices, ingredients, or you might not like their product after you've tried it.

In order to run your business with integrity, you can't be in it just for the money. I would like to make money, but nothing beats my audience's experience. You need to make sure you are delivering valuable content that is interesting, whether or not your visitors buy something from one of your affiliates. Your number one priority is to weave affiliates into your content and to be transparent and authentic in whatever you are promoting.

7 Affiliate Marketing Strategies All Blogs Must Follow

Now that you know how affiliate marketing works, here are some strategies that every blog needs to follow.

21. Add links to posts that perform well.

Go back and find the posts that were the most popular and weave affiliate links into their content. If you are still getting traffic to these posts, then it would be great if you can make money from those engagements.

You need to make sure that the links feel natural and not like you are placing promo links just "anywhere."

22. Make videos for your top affiliates.

It would be a great idea to add helpful videos to your affiliate posts. Most bloggers know that videos are extremely popular right now. Videos can help show the buyer what to expect if they do decide to buy what you are promoting. If it is a great program, service, or product, seeing it in action will make them want to buy it.

It's just like scrolling through Facebook and seeing a cooking video that makes you stop and watch. You get sucked in and think, "Wow, I can do that." Before you know it, you are running to the store to buy the ingredients to make that recipe.

If you appear in the video, it will make your audience more familiar with you. You want your audience to feel comfortable around you. You want them to trust you and feel like they know you. Sometimes there isn't any better way to do this than a video.

23. Make dedicated posts for your top affiliates.

Your readers will buy a product faster if they see the value that it brings into your life. The best way to show them this is by a dedicated blog that details one affiliate and all the reasons why you love them, including ways these products will make the reader's life so much better.

You can do this with review style posts. When a person reads about something, the more they are likely to think: "This sounds helpful. I think I will try it."

You only need to do this for your top affiliates, since it won't be worth your time and effort to make blog posts for affiliates that just bring in a couple of bucks each month.

24. Make a resource page.

You might be familiar with a "resource page," since most blogs will have them nowadays. Basically, it is a roundup of your favorite courses, subscriptions, apps, services, or products that you think your readers will like, too. These are things that you get value from. These will be your best performing affiliate links.

Don't stop there. Many people tend to have only one resource page, but you can have as many as you would like. If you have multiple niches, think about breaking up your content into many pages that have been targeted to cover specific niches, versus only one page that is general.

25. Place affiliate links on social media.

There are many different social media sites out there, so why not use them all?

• Twitter

You can tweet about why you love your affiliate. Remember to tag them and use their affiliate link. It's that simple.

• Facebook

You can post videos and photos of your affiliates on your page, with an announcement about time-sensitive enrollments or sales for your affiliates.

Videos are wonderful: you can do unboxing videos and put it on various channels; you can create a tutorial or video about a certain topic and then link it to products in your Facebook shop in the caption. You could even do a Facebook Live and mention any affiliates if you think it is appropriate.

• Instagram

You can add affiliate links to your stories, your favorite things, your highlight reel, or static posts. You don't need to overdo it, because you want to stay authentic and not have your feed look like thousands of billboards.

Adding links every now and then is a great way to reach more people while sharing helpful recommendations.

- **Pinterest**

You can "pin" things that will either send your audience to a direct link where they can buy a product, or to your blog post where you have written about your affiliate.

You should have pictures so you will stand out, and where you can, offer a discount or special deal by using a link.

Make sure to schedule these posts by using Tailwind.

You need to remember that on all social media platforms you have to use #affiliate for transparency, or indicate the affiliate relationship when posting an affiliate link by saying "thank you" beside the link.

On all platforms, you can use "share threads" to get engagement with your videos and posts. This will help show the algorithm that people like your content and this will help expand your reach.

26. Put affiliate links inside emails.

You can follow up regular emails with a wrap-up weekly email where you can remind people about what you loved about that week, along with some updates on new blog posts.

On Sundays, you can send out a list of emails where you include some affiliate links for services and products that you love and are currently using. These emails need to be personal. You need to talk about your life, you, and what you are loving, feeling, reading, eating, and doing.

This list is meant to give your readers value, while building your relationship with them and earning their trust, so you can inspire others to live a better, healthier life.

This means that three times each week, you have the opportunity to make money from affiliate marketing, while also providing your readers with product recommendations and value that could solve a problem they might be having in their life. Plus, you can give them tricks, tips, and fun updates.

27. Send emails that highlight one affiliate company.

Once your readers have signed up for your emails, you can officially begin sending them emails.

Pick a day of the week that works best for you and send out an email that features only one affiliate service or product that you are currently using and have fallen in love with. It might be a new product or just one your affiliate is promoting. Just make sure you have tested and tried this product and can give a true recommendation. You can also choose a new affiliate, so you can see how interested your readers are with them.

Make sure that these emails are just promoting one thing, so you don't distract your readers or give them too many calls to action. If you give a reader too many choices, they usually don't make any.

Give your readers ways to opt-out of emails. Be realistic, some people will get annoyed and won't want to get all of your emails anymore. Make it easy for them to opt-out of certain emails. You want to keep your people happy.

Some email systems don't have this functionality; ConvertKit makes this very easy to do.

Affiliate Marketing Networks: Which One?

Let's find out how to find the right affiliate network that will work best for you and your niche and we aren't talking about Amazon.

• ClickBank

ClickBank isn't just another affiliate network. It is a marketplace for affiliates and people who create products, so people can make money together without having agreements or a lot of paperwork.

ClickBank is a middleman between people who create digital products like music, videos, and e-books, and people who want to sell these products.

Being an affiliate marketer, you can create your unique affiliate link for thousands of products and begin to drive traffic to begin making money. You get to see your earnings in real-time.

It is free to join and there isn't a screening process. There aren't any complicated metrics. It is just a simplified network that is open to anybody who wants to try it.

- **ShareASale**

This company was founded in 2000. It is an affiliate network from Chicago, Illinois. ShareASale will pay a commission to affiliates based on their sales. You can choose from over 2500 programs that let you earn commissions.

The website features over 2500 merchants that offer many different services and products. Being an affiliate, you will select any of the merchants and try to make direct sales to their websites. The merchants will then pay you a commission for the sales that resulted from the affiliate's referrals. You get to decide the merchant that you would like to promote and ways you would want to promote them. You can log into the website and check the merchant's earnings and stats in real-time.

- **AvantLink**

This company has been in business for ten years and it is still improving its platform. AvantLink has been recognized as the fastest-growing entrepreneurial business in its field. It constantly strives for excellence and has an intense focus on quality instead of quantity.

If you have joined an affiliate network and later didn't like it, AvantLink removes this problem by giving you detailed overviews of all the merchant's programs before you join. By doing this, you don't have to worry about signing up for its program. You will be able to see information about the company, its products, and its affiliate program. This is the best feature for new affiliates who are worried about jumping into a program.

- **Rakuten Marketing**

Formerly known as LinkShare, Rakuten Marketing claims to be the largest affiliate marketing network out there today. It offers e-commerce, securities, banking, travel, e-books, media, and online marketing services.

Rakuten Marketing's system is always learning, in order to constantly bring customers into better focus. By analyzing its data, the company has a good understanding of consumers: where they are going, where they have been, what they value, and who they are. These insights, along with multi-channeled data, allow for intelligent optimization across all campaigns, for better effectiveness. The company gives its clients complete visibility and access to its platform.

Rakuten Marketing works with over 150,000 publishers around the world, as well as the biggest brands. Intelligence and insight get shared between publishing partners and advertisers and their joint success comes from working together.

- **CJ.com**

This company was previously called Commission Junction. You can find thousands of products on its website to make money off of. This affiliate is great for bloggers to connect with affiliate programs that get offered by thousands of online brands. The best part is that you don't need any exclusive training to learn how to use this network. Just sign up for a free account and begin exploring.

After you have signed up, complete your profile to make sure you get fast approval for CJ's affiliate program. Now, you can click on links to search for your niche or you can click on categories to browse new programs. You get paid through a check or by direct deposit.

- **FlexOffers**

FlexOffers will connect you with many reputable brand name companies that you can be an affiliate for. It has over 12,000 affiliate programs and adds new ones every day. FlexOffers has a wide range of programs for just about every niche out there.

To sign up, just go to the website and begin. Even if your blog is just beginning to grow, you will still be able to join, as long as you explain how you will promote products. Be as detailed as possible about your traffic sources, this gives you a better chance of being accepted into the program.

- **OfferVault**

This affiliate marketing website can find you cost-per-action offers from more than 60 affiliate networks.

Categories get listed for every search term that you enter, along with all of the relevant information on those offers made by the merchants. You will find all the offers that are available for your niche, so you can compare them to other networks.

OfferVault earns money by collecting monthly fees from the network for listing their offers.

Amazon Affiliate Marketing Made Easy

To make sure that you do well using the Amazon Associates program, let's go over some of the best tricks in the business.

1. Place links to products within your content.

Most income made from Amazon's affiliate program will come from basic text links. This means that you will hyperlink certain words in your text that people can click on that will take them to a product page on Amazon. You want to make sure this fits in with your niche and what you are talking about in your blog post. It's going to seem really odd if you are talking about losing weight and then you have a random paragraph that says, "Hey, check out this cool drone."

2. Turn images into clickable affiliate links.

Of course, the image should be of the actual product. These are the next best affiliate links to use on your website.

3. Add links to Amazon as often as you can.

The more links you have on your site, the more likely somebody will be to click on them. Don't wait until the very end to place your affiliate link. By the end, they should have been given numerous opportunities to click through to Amazon.

4. Product reviews do the best.

Doing some quality product reviews of things that relate to your niche is a great way to get a higher click-through rate and more sales. You want to make sure the review is very high quality, though. Ideally, you will want to get in contact with the company and have them send you a demo item to do the review on, but this takes more effort and won't work if you are just starting out. You can still do a review on things that you have actually bought and used.

5. Work during the holidays.

When do people buy the most? During the holidays. One Amazon affiliate made between $550 and $1000 each day during the week after Thanksgiving. Not all holidays payout this well, but typically you will make more money during gift-giving times of the year.

6. Place a "Buy Now" button in your posts.

You can do this easily with the EasyAzon plugin, but if you don't want to spend the money on that, you can insert a button yourself and make it an affiliate link.

7. Post articles about recurring deals.

If you want to be able to share posts about products that are on sale more often, the best way to do this is with a "weekly deals" post. So, you will publish a post each week with the best deals for items within your niche and then use all of the other tactics that we have covered.

8. Do a monthly bestseller list.

Amazon keeps an updated "bestsellers" list, so all you would have to do is post a blog each month and mention their list.

9. Just get people to visit Amazon.

One affiliate says that 30% of her earnings come from people who made a purchase on Amazon and she happened to be the person who sent them to Amazon. For example, she said that through one of her links, she sold a $5000 watch and made a $400 commission, but she doesn't have a website or link that talks about watches. When a person goes to Amazon from one of your links, you will get a percentage of whatever they buy for the following 24 hours, or 30 days if they add something to their cart. So, all you need to do is get them to click on one of your links.

Proven Strategies: The Amazon Affiliate Website That Makes $20k/Month

For this case study, I want to introduce you to 10beasts.com. This company has figured out how to make big money with the Amazon Associates program. Luqman Khan, the guy behind this website is big into technology, and it originally started out as a top 10 website.

When you go to the site, you will notice that it is very simple. It doesn't confuse you and it is very straightforward. It also only has about ten to fifteen pages. When you click on a post, there is a well-defined sidebar, which is something that is becoming obsolete in a lot of website themes. Another thing Luqman has figured out is how to keyword his title. The way he does that is by frequently using the year in the title: it gives him access to untouched traffic, and he updates his product reviews each year.

He also makes sure that he uses the main keyword of his blog post several times throughout the post, and definitely within the first 100 words. He also links out to other authoritative websites.

When it comes down to showing the list of the best whatever-he-is-talking-about in his post, he uses a table instead of listing things. Everything on the table is hyperlinked to another place in the article where you can read more about it, and he has the link for the Amazon page. All of the tables he uses can easily be created through plugins with WordPress. He also makes sure he shows the pros and cons of items, because people want to hear the truth.

So, he has figured out the best way to draw people in through the use of good keywords, and then he provides them with amazing content. This means that he has more people clicking through on his Amazon affiliate links and purchasing items. The great thing is that they don't have to buy that specific item for him to get the commission. As long as they buy something after clicking on his link, he gets a seven percent commission on the sale.

Chapter 4: Blogging Secret #3: E-Commerce & Dropshipping

The next way you can make money with your blog is through e-commerce or dropshipping. These require a more hands-on approach and you will definitely have to spend some money. This is also a type of monetization that won't work for everybody. There are some blog niches that simply don't provide you an easy item that you can sell. For example, if you choose a niche in finance, selling actual products is probably not a good idea. You could sell other things like books and classes that you create yourself, which we will talk about later, but you can't dropship or outsource items. But, if you are blogging about sports, then you can easily sell sports equipment. So, we're going to take a look at the different ways to get started with e-commerce and dropshipping.

Shopify Hacks You Need to Know

For most people who decide to get into e-commerce, Shopify's embedded capabilities helps to meet all of their needs. First, though, everything we are going to talk about in this section applies to every other section in this chapter. How you can use blogging to help your

Shopify business will help you with any other e-commerce or dropshipping business you create.

Shopify's embedded capabilities are also free and easy to start using and can help you get the most out of your store and your blog. First, you have to add your blog to your Shopify account. Go to the admin area and click on: "Online Store." Then choose: "Blog Posts." Then you will click: "Manage Blogs" and then: "Add Blog." You will then fill in the title of your blog. You can also have multiple blogs on one Shopify site.

Now you can write your blog post. You want to keep it relevant to your Shopify store. As we have talked about a lot, keep it contained in a niche. It will attract shoppers and keep them coming back.

Then you need to decide how you are going to manage your comments. You can either disable them, moderate them, or let them be automatically published. I would suggest moderating them. This means you have to approve them before they get published. This cuts down on rude comments and spam.

You also need to pick the right tags. This is how readers are going to find your blog. Then decide which social media buttons you are going to allow. They include Instagram, Pinterest, Twitter, Facebook, and others.

So how do you get people to come to your Shopify store? Here are a few tips:

1. A referral program.

You can generate traffic and sales by putting together a referral program for your store. An easy way to do this is with Shopify Affiliate Software. You can provide people a link to promote your site through online platforms and email.

2. Image SEO.

You can optimize your images to help them show up in searches more often. You will want to make sure that your images are properly tagged for social media and they should be compressed so that it improves the speed of the page. Shopify gives you the ability to edit image names and text so that you can create compelling descriptions.

3. Test prices.

You can split-test prices (also known as A/B testing) on Shopify for free and this is one of the best ways to figure out what people are willing to pay for certain items. Having the wrong price can end up sinking your store before it has even started. Using the Qbot Shopify app gives you the chance to split test prices, but you should plan out your tests over a certain period of time instead of testing everything all at once.

4. Trial run.

Have an idea that you can't wait to get started? You can see how well it will work on Shopify for free. Their store builder provides you with a free fourteen-day trial, but make sure that you have your supplier and stock sorted out. You can get the store up and running quickly, and during those free fourteen days, you can figure out if it is going to work for you or not.

5. Digital content.

Shopify also allows you to sell your expertise. So, if you don't want to sell physical products, you can sell digital downloads like webinars, e-books, worksheets, and so on.

With this in mind, go check out Shopify and see if it will work for you, (but after you have finished reading the rest of this book.)

Dropshipping Tips and Tricks

You may or may not have heard the term dropshipping before. If not, it is simply a way to sell things without having to have physical products on hand. You post things for sale on eBay or Amazon, and when somebody buys it, you go to another site and place the order for the item and put in the other person's shipping information. The dropshipper then sends the item to the person who bought it. But there is a little more to it than this.

The biggest plus with dropshipping is that it doesn't require any up-front investments. You don't have to buy products until somebody buys something from you. This may make dropshipping sound like it is a zero risk, high-reward business, and it basically is, but there are some risks associated with it. So, let's move into the risk and reward of dropshipping.

Advantage #1: Zero Capital Required

You can start a dropshipping business with zero money because you don't have to buy any products.

Advantage #2: Work Anywhere

You don't have to have a physical location, and you don't even have to be at home. As long as you have your phone or computer, you can work from anywhere.

Advantage #3: Scalability

It doesn't matter if you are selling phone cases or large pieces of furniture, the amount of work you have to put in is going to be the same. All you have to do is give your supplier the order information. The only limits are the limits that your supplier has.

Advantage #4: Endless Number of Products

Since you don't have to purchase any products, that means you can offer a wide variety of products and allow your sales data and blog posts to drive your business.

Disadvantage #1: High Risk

While you don't have to invest money, it is still high risk. The physical aspects of your business will be completely out of your hands. While you still have to tell your customers that you have stock, quick shipping and handling, and high quality products, you don't have any real control over these things. All of this is controlled by your supplier. It is common for a person to sell something and then go to their supplier to find out that they are out of stock. Most people will plan for this and have more than one dropshipper if this happens. But it is a risk that you might not be able to plan for.

Disadvantage #2: Low-Profit Margins

It doesn't take too much to get started with dropshipping, so it has become a very crowded business model, especially over the last few years. This means sellers have to be able to stand out in order to generate substantial revenue. But, you are starting with a blog, which may be just what you need to stand out from your competition.

Disadvantage #3: Slow Shipping Times

Shipping times are one of the biggest factors buyers look at with online shopping. Before you know it, Amazon will have drones delivering everything to people in about an hour. When you dropship your orders, the dropshippers will ship a lot slower than if you have control over it.

Alright, now that you know the advantages and disadvantages, let's move into the different types of dropshipping.

1. Dropshipping from suppliers.

This is the most common form of dropshipping. There are various suppliers that you can use, and you can negotiate your business deal before you start to list their products on Amazon or eBay. This way, you can establish a relationship with an actual supplier, unlike working with AliExpress. But finding a good supplier can sometimes be hard. It can take months to find the right supplier for you. There is also a lot of room for error.

2. Dropshipping from online retailers.

This is what is known as the arbitrage dropshipping model. The seller will take a look at the prices of items on different retailers, typically either Overstock, Target, Walmart, AliExpress, eBay, or Amazon. Let's say somebody finds an item for sale on Amazon for

$50 and the same item on eBay for $60. He would then exploit this arbitrage and make a profit by selling it on eBay and ordering it from Amazon.

This doesn't require you to establish a relationship with actual suppliers. When the person buys something from you, you go to Amazon and place the order and ship it to your buyer. This form of dropshipping is not very sustainable. Competition drives the price, so prices have a chance to change drastically in a short amount of time. Plus, this form of dropshipping kind of looks bad. A person orders something from eBay but then gets something in an Amazon box. Most marketplaces are trying to get rid of this form of dropshipping, so this may not be a good idea.

3. Dropshipping with Amazon FBA.

With this type of dropshipping, you would ship a bulk supply of your product to Amazon's warehouses. Amazon stores the product and then ships it out when a person orders it. You can also sell on other sites using Amazon's Fulfillment by Amazon (FBA) account. This incentivizes sellers to make sales on Amazon through a discounted shipping and handling rate. This isn't purely dropshipping, though, because you will need to purchase the product beforehand and ship it to Amazon's warehouses.

How Do You Start?

You don't need to quit your job first. Start your dropshipping and blog business on the side, and then once you have become established and are making revenue, you can quit your job. For example, Pierre Omidyar, the founder of eBay, didn't quit his job as a programmer until eBay generated an income that was more than his salary.

It's okay if you have zero experience, but you should still know the basics of bookkeeping, finances, and business registration. This will keep you from running into any problems once your business starts to take off. You don't have to do this right off the bat, but as soon as you have started to make about $500 each month, you should take some time to look into these four things:

1. Create the simplest form of a business in your country. For the US, this is a "Sole Proprietorship."

2. Create a business credit card and bank account.

3. Create a business PayPal account.

4. Learn e-commerce bookkeeping or find a professional to help you.

When it comes to finding products to sell, the best place to turn to is Alibaba.com. Here you will find lots of different suppliers and products. You can contact several suppliers about the same product and figure out which one is willing to give you the best price. Once you have decided who you are going to dropship with, and hashed out your deal, then you can list the item for sale on whatever marketplace you choose. You can also make a marketplace on your website.

Be ready for questions. People will want to know more about your product, so you will need to know how to answer their questions. You may have to go back to the supplier and ask them. In fact, I would suggest doing just that, so that you give your customers the right answer.

Once you make your first sale, you have to place your order with the supplier. The first time you do this, you may be afraid of screwing something up. You will go back to your supplier's site and send them the agreed-upon money for the item and give them the shipping information for the buyer. Once they get the money, they will send the product out to the buyer. You will then want to let the buyer know their order is on its way.

One last piece of advice for dropshipping is to go with products that have a price of $100 to $300. This gives you the biggest profit margin and people feel more comfortable buying things in this price range. Any higher, and people may think they are getting ripped off, and any lower, people may think the quality is bad.

Masters of the Marketplace (eBay, Amazon and More)

The next way to make money through e-commerce and your blog is to use different marketplaces. These include eBay, Amazon, and many more. Some people who sell on these marketplaces don't have a blog, while others do. To get the most from marketplaces, it is best to have a blog, because it is a great way to drive traffic to your stores. Linking to a store on another site is also cheaper than paying for a web page that has a store. Let's look at some ways to master these various marketplaces.

Most people will source their products from China, and this can take some time because you will want to get samples and see who has the best quality products. But the first thing you need to do is figure out what your first product is going to be. I'm going to share with you three product ideas. These are by no means the only options you have, and your products will also depend on what your blog niche is, because you want to make sure that they go together.

The first product is silicone ice cube trays. This product has a lot of revenue coming in. The top sellers of this product are bringing in 30k each month. It should also be easy to import and it shouldn't cause any problems. There is also a gap where people are having a hard time with their lids staying on the trays, so you could find a better quality product to offer. There are also products you could start selling that fit with this.

The second product is moth traps. Again, they have a good amount of revenue, not as much as the last product, but still averaging around 9k each month. Moth traps are also small and light, so this product is easy to import as well. There is also a gap that you can fix by improving upon the trap itself. It can also be easily bundled with other products.

The last product is a collapse laundry basket, which also has healthy revenue. These can also be easily shipped because they are collapsible. There are also ways to improve these.

As you can see, when it comes to figuring out what to sell, there are three main things you need to think about. First off, is the product going to make a decent amount of revenue? Second, how easy is it going to be to import and ship? Third, is there a way that you can improve things so that you can stand out from the competition?

Now, you are probably wondering where you can find your products to sell on eBay and Amazon. As I've said, most people will source their items from China because they can get them for a lot cheaper there, which gives you a bigger profit margin. But you don't have to source from China.

There are some people who simply go to places like Goodwill. Yes, I said Goodwill. If you've not been, it's a secondhand store where you can find clothing, houseware, and electronics. The crazy thing is, you can sometimes find unopened items and clothing that has barely, if ever, been worn. Other types of thrift stores are also a good idea. These places get leftover products that didn't get sold, and they sell them for less than half of their regular retail price.

Another option is to go to flea markets. You'd be amazed at what you can find at flea markets. There is a lot of stuff you may have to sort through, and there are people who know what they have, so you won't be able to talk them down in price, but sooner or later you will be able to find things that you can resell for a profit.

You can also look for online and brick and mortar shops that are having a sale or even going out of business. These are great times to stock up on items and still be able to make a profit on them when you resell them.

Now, remember, we're talking about making money through your blog. The first thing you need to do is figure out what things you can sell that fit in with your niche blog. When you do, you can funnel your readers to your shop on Amazon or eBay by placing a call-to-action at the bottom of all of your blog posts. As long as you make sure that you share calls to action regularly, and you constantly remind your readers about your shop, you can easily make money by selling on eBay or Amazon.

Etsy: Shine at Selling Your Own Products

Unlike the other e-commerce outlets that we have talked about, Etsy requires a more hands-on approach. Etsy is where people share their handmade items and various services, which range from clothing to tarot card readings. But getting sales is most of the time the hardest part, and that is where your blogging comes in.

Blogging to market your Etsy shop is one of the best ways to market for Etsy, instead of spending money on Etsy ads that may not work. I'm going to be honest with you right now; a lot of people will tell you that making money with your blog is easier than making money on Etsy. But, having a blog will enable you to make more Etsy sales. Here's an example of how a blog can help out: let's say a woman has worked hard for two years to establish herself on Etsy and is making $2500 a month in sales, so she decides to take a vacation. When she comes back, she switches out of vacation mode and all she gets is crickets. She is no longer making the sales she has made before.

Now, if this same woman had a blog, things would work a little bit differently. Before she heads out on vacation, she sends a message out to her readers letting them know what she is up to, so they know what is going on. Then, instead of turning off vacation mode as soon as she gets home, she sends out some messages to her followers. She tells them about her vacation and how she bought some supplies and is starting to make a new line for her Etsy store.

She chooses to put together a giveaway on her blog and other social media sites. In a week, she messages her readers asking if they want to be a part of her giveaway. The giveaway is a huge success. Once she picks a winner, she holds a flash sale for everybody that entered the giveaway for two days. A third of the people who entered buy something during this time. So instead of hearing crickets when she comes back from vacation, her shop is up and running again.

You can't rely on Etsy to make you successful. You have to go where the buyers are, and this means social media and blogs. You tell them through those outlets about what is going on with your Etsy shop. But when you choose a blog, you are basically creating a trap for shoppers. You have created one place where people can go to get updates from you, which is easier than them having to chase you around on several different sites.

You have their complete attention on your blog, and you post things that relate to the products you sell on Etsy. Here are some examples of Etsy sellers who became successful because of their blog.

A woman named Dana Fox created the blog called Wonder Forest. On Etsy, she sells phone cases and accessories. On her blog, she shares life hacks and tips in order to make your life fun and easy.

Liz Marie created a blog where she talks about interior design. On her Etsy shop, she sells vintage décor.

As you can see, blogs can make an average Etsy shop successful, and help you to bring in more money without a bunch of extra work on Etsy.

Proven Strategies: How One Woman Makes $40k/Month on Amazon

In this success story, one woman went from working a job and going to school full-time, to making around $40,000 each month on Amazon. It all started for her when she and her boyfriend took a class called ASM. This class sparked something inside of the woman to start an online business, mainly because she could do it while still working and going to school.

When it came time to pick her first product, she decided to go with something lightweight and affordable, because she didn't have extra money to spend on something big. She chose a konjac sponge, which is a beauty product. She did pretty well selling this product. She also did all of the other aspects of the business herself, like her business logo design and so on. The anonymous woman in this example says she only invested around $300 in this first product. She sourced this item from China, where each unit only cost her ten cents.

This first product had made it to $3,000 a month in earnings, when she started to think about her next product. Instead of focusing on the long-term at this time, she was just looking to see what would make her the most money. With time, she learned to look long-term and focus on building a brand that she could take off of Amazon and sell on her own website. Her trendy second product was 3-D fiber mascara. It brought her $5,000 a month.

At this point, the woman knew she wanted to go for a product that would bring in more money, instead of products that can be sold at a cheap price. Her advice is to go with something that is worth more than $20. This will give you better product margins. Plus, it gives you a better chance of making the product unique.

With time, she started having problems getting her products because she was sourcing them from China. At one point, her product got caught up in customs for a month, which hurt her on Amazon because she didn't have anything to sell. So, she made a transition to where she is now. She looked at Amazon and tried to figure out what she should do differently, using herself as an example to figure out what consumers bought on Amazon. The woman realized that waist trainers were the main thing that she bought on Amazon, and it was a very specific niche.

As she made this move, she started to look at ways to save herself money and make sure her business wasn't damaged by returns. That's when she turned to social media to market herself and make sure that people measured themselves before they bought her product. She turned to YouTube, and this helped her create traction, because she kept everything very niche and focused on waist trainers. She also used Facebook and has a private Facebook group for people who have bought her products. She used these social media outlets to save money on ads, and the more people she attracted to these outlets, the more sales she started to make on Amazon.

She also made sure her product was better quality than was otherwise available on Amazon. It was also a product that she trusted. With her faith in the product and her social media marketing, she was able to up her sales on Amazon, until she reached $40,000 a month. She has now expanded and started her own website as well, and she suggests that should be something people aim for when it comes to e-commerce.

Chapter 5: Blogging Secret #4: Expert Info-Products

The next way we are going to look at making money with your blog is through selling info-products. This means you are going to have to establish yourself as an authority figure and then create something that people will want to buy to learn from.

Sell Your Expertise

Before you start trying to sell info-products, you have to show you are an expert. It doesn't matter whether you feel like an expert or not, you have to make your possible clients feel as if you are, otherwise, you won't sell a thing.

Some fields have qualifications that show people that they are an expert. For example, you could be a registered dietician and that automatically makes you seem like an expert in diet and nutrition. Other areas of expertise aren't so easy. But right now, I want you to think about the people you view as experts in your chosen niche. Now, what if you had the combined knowledge of these people? This doesn't mean knowing everything they know, but having a general understanding of the topics they cover. Would you feel as if you were an expert? Probably.

Write down those people who came to mind, and then write down their most important works. Once you have figured out their body of work, you will choose a couple of those to focus on. This is the knowledge you need to learn. Take some time to study up on these things, and make lists or mindmaps to help you learn the topics.

You don't have to be able to quote everything that is covered, but you do want a decent understanding of the information. You want to understand it enough that you can confidently answer questions about it.

Then, start putting yourself out there. Publish regular blog posts and diversify the content that you share. Start looking to get added to speaking events. This puts your face out there as well. An important thing to remember is, once you start becoming more popular and more established, don't become arrogant. You want to stay tasteful and respectful. If you start becoming cocky, condescending, or rude, you will lose your status as an expert.

Lastly, make sure you create original content. I understand that almost everything has been covered before by someone else, but you can put your own spin on things. Make sure you never plagiarize another. You can let others inspire you, but always come up with your own blog posts and so forth.

Kickass Info-Products and How to Sell Them

So, you want to monetize your knowledge. Well, the first way to do that is through info-products. Basically, an info-product is something that has been created from one or more sources to meet a certain purpose. The format of these products can be video, audio, written, or a combination of all of them. These are the seven main types of info-products:

> 1. **E-books** – These are digital books that people can read on devices. This is a type of passive income, because all you will need to do is promote it once it is published.
>
> 2. **Phone applications** – These are apps that people use that allow them to interact with information. This requires a lot of technical know-how, or you will have to hire a person to

make it for you, which can cost a lot. It could, however, make you some passive income, depending on what your app is about.

3. **Membership sites** – This is a website people pay to be a part of to get regular content that they can't get on the free version of the site. This requires a hands-on approach and is not a form of passive income.

4. **Virtual summits** – This is like an online conference. A person will get access to different webinars and videos created by various experts. This will take time to put together, and requires a more hands-on approach. This does not make passive income, because it takes place at a certain time.

5. **Webinars** – Short videos that are shared live that focus on a small part of an expert's bigger picture. They can be replayed at any time when a person purchases access to the webinar, so this makes passive income.

6. **Online courses** – This is a course that has been created that people can take online to learn about something. It takes a lot of time to create, but it makes passive income once it is up and running, requiring only promotion.

7. **Workbooks and templates** – This is another book that a person can fill in. It is structured in a way that helps the customer learn something. Again, this involves passive income, only promoting is required.

Now you have to figure out which type of info-product you should create. To figure that out, ask yourself these questions:

1.   How much time are you willing to spend on creating your product? And how much effort? An online course takes a lot more time than a webinar.

2.   Do you want to make one thing and sell it over and over, or do you want to create content on a regular basis?

3.   How much money do you want to bring in versus the effort?

4.   How much experience and knowledge do you have in your niche and do you want to partner with other experts?

5.   What does your audience want and are they already buying things?

6.   How many tools do you know how to use and are you ready to learn new things?

So how do you sell these products online? Here are some important steps to take to do so:

1. Who is the target market and what problem are you going to help them solve?

You will see this time and time again in this book, but it is the first step on almost everything you will do, when it comes to monetizing your blog. You must stay within your niche, so within that, who are you going to try to sell to and what is it that they need help with? If you are in the fitness world, are you selling to people who need to lose weight, or people who need to bulk up? Those are two very different types of people, so you have to know your target market and what they need help with.

2. Research your competition.

Look to see what is already available for your target market. Then you will need to figure out how you can position yourself within all of that. ClickBank is a great place to see what is already out there, and it is a place where you can sell your products as well.

3. What is your big idea?

This is what people are going to be paying for. This is your promise, so to speak. Going back to the fitness example, there are lots of different big ideas that you can share. Maybe you have a workout plan that helps bodybuilders gain lots of muscle in a short time. Basically, you want to know what you are going to sell and how you are going to make that stand out against the competition, so you have to make it fun and exciting.

4. Come up with your product marketing.

Don't make the product yet. You need to sit down and figure out how you are going to market your product. This will include the benefits of your product and success stories that your product can bring. This is all how you are going to sell your product once you are ready to share it.

5. How are you going to share your product?

This is probably the most overwhelming step. This is where you need to decide how you are going to get your product out there. The easiest way to handle this without getting overwhelmed is to focus on a single platform at first. I would suggest starting with Facebook Ads because it is one of the easiest platforms to use and will bring you a lot of revenue.

6. Create your product.

Now you can make the product. Depending on what product you choose, this could take a few days to several months to do. But, I also want to say, you should have fun with this step. This is where you get to be creative, instead of dealing with all the technical parts. Once your product is created, you can launch on your chosen site.

7. Keep an eye on your sales.

Once you have launched your product, you need to keep an eye on the metrics and see how it is doing. You may find that you have to change your distribution avenues, landing pages, or ads. You shouldn't just "let it be" because that is the quickest way to lose money. Babysit it and adjust things as you see fit.

E-Book Launching and Marketing Secrets

Selling e-books is no small feat. One side of the playing field is people telling you it's easy and they made hundreds, if not thousands, of dollars overnight. On the other side are people telling you that you have to market, market, market and sales won't happen overnight. Neither one is inherently wrong or right. But the one thing the people who made money overnight aren't telling you is that they did market. They probably put a bunch of blood, sweat, and tears into their book and the marketing before it ever launched. This means that marketing is really the most important thing in making money with your e-books. We're going to look at some of the best practices.

1. Consider who your audience is.

The first thing you have to do is figure out who your audience is and what your book is going to provide them. This is going to also center around your blog niche. Remember, these are all ways for you to make money through your blog. If you are writing a blog about investing, then your readers are going to want a book from you that centers around investing and not a cookbook of your grandmother's favorite recipes. Also, think about how you are going to prove to your readers that they should trust the information in your book. How do they know you know what you're talking about?

2. Build a landing page.

Next, you've got to figure out how you are going to get people to actually see your book and want to buy it. This is where a landing page with a free offering comes in. You want to give them something of value and also be able to fulfill any promises you have or will make.

If you plan on staying in the blogging game, any form of deceit is going to end up costing you a lot. Word will spread fast that you don't deliver, and people will stay away. If you use MailChimp for your email list, this company offers a landing page of sorts. On that landing page, it needs to say something along the lines of "Sign up today and get my free ..." This free thing needs to be something your readers are going to want to have. Maybe you have some videos that you could sell as a free beginner's course about something. Or you could offer a PDF that includes helpful information. The important thing is that it will be something that your readers will actually find valuable, and they won't feel like they have been cheated, while you are also not giving away a lot of material for free.

3. Create a compelling call-to-action.

Think about your niche, how are you going to draw your audience in? If your niche is within the fitness and health realm, is there some secret workout that you have created or know about that few others know about? If you help with relationships, do you have some tools to offer your audience that they won't be able to find elsewhere?

This is what you are going to place at the end of your blog posts that have a link to your MailChimp landing page. This is how you are going to get people to sign up for your email list, so that they stay up-to-date and you have people to market to when it comes time to launch your book.

4. Create a conversation.

You have a growing email list now, so it is important to get to know those people. You now have to send them regular emails so that they know you're still alive. It's these emails that are going to help you build a rapport with them. Let them know about your upcoming articles, but also engage with them. Ask them questions. Things like, who are you, what things would you like to see me cover, or is there something that you are struggling with? This shows your readers that you care and that you want to help them. This will also help to build trust.

5. Begin writing your book.

This probably seems too far down on the list, but you want to make sure you have people to sell your book to before you write your book. Now, I can't tell you what you need to write or how to write it. That is all up to you. This is probably one of the hardest parts of the process, because for everything else you can follow a system others have used, but writing a book is something personal. It will likely take you months to do, and then you have to edit it. But, I trust that you can do this as long as you have figured out your audience and everything I asked you to do in step one.

6. Marketing your book.

This is the most important part. Now, you can do this through the email list you have created, and that's why we created the email list. If you are using MailChimp, you can come up with a campaign to send out to your subscribers that highlights different parts of your book and explains why it would be valuable to your subscribers. I would suggest making this a week-long campaign that goes all the way up to your publishing date. This will get you presales. It may also cost some of your subscribers, but that's okay. Not everybody will be at a point in their life to take a chance on you, so buying a book might not fit into where they are. But you should also make some sales.

Through these steps, you should have a solid foundation for creating and selling your e-book. It's also important to ask your readers to leave you a review if they liked the book. Reviews are what helps you place higher on Amazon. Then people who have bought, read and liked your book will share it with other people. This should become a snowball effect on the sales of your book.

Teach It: Selling Courses and Webinars

The next way to make money online by sharing your expertise is through webinars and courses. This is probably one of the hardest options because coming up with a course, creating it, and then selling it, can seem quite daunting. But I am going to talk about some of the best strategies to use to make sure you are able to successfully create and sell a course online.

1. Make sure you know what you want to teach.

This shouldn't just be an idea of what you want to teach or simply your niche. This means what you want to provide a person. What are they going to be able to do after your course that they couldn't do before it? Nobody has ever woken up one morning thinking, "I want to buy an online course today." No. That's not going to happen. People don't buy courses just to buy courses. They buy the courses to get a specific outcome, so you want to make sure that you know what outcome your course is going to give them.

2. Coming up with a good price.

This is probably the hardest part, aside from making the actual course. Most people will undercharge on their course, mainly because they don't think their information is valuable. Their content is just fine; they are simply lacking confidence. As a general rule of thumb, $100 should be the lowest you should price your courses.

This may or may not sound like a lot to you, but research has found that people are more likely to buy and finish an online course if they are priced over $100 than under $100. It goes back to the whole idea of: "You get what you pay for," as well as the fact that the more money a person has invested in something, the more likely they are to finish it. If you have a price in mind, chances are, if you double it, you will be closer to a good price.

A lot of people have undercharged and not done well, but when they go to re-release, they double the price and they start doing better. Another way to figure out the price is to double what you think it's worth and then add 50%.

3. Figure out what goals you want to meet with your course.

Now, the best way to sell your online course is to have an established email list. Those people on the email list should be people interested in your topic, and when you launch the course, you sell it to them. So, figuring out your goals will let you know how many people you need to make sure you have on your email list before you launch.

Here's an example of how you can figure this out. Let's say your goal is to make $10,000 in income. The conversion rate for the number of people who will buy from your email list is about two percent, and let's say your course price is $300. You then would take that information to figure out how many people you need on your email list. In this example, you would need 1700 people on your email list, in order to reach your goal of $10,000 at a two percent conversion rate.

4. Build your email list.

Now that you know how many people you need, you need to build your email list. There are a lot of different ways to build an email list. Basically, all you need to do is figure out what you can give away in return for an email address. You've seen things like this on websites, I'm sure. A pop-up comes up telling you if you sign up you get a free copy of an e-book or a free course. This is just one example of how to get subscribers, but it is a very effective way, because people like to get free things.

5. Come up with an outline and create your content.

While this may be what you want to start with, it should really be closer to the bottom of your list. You want to make sure that you will be successful on your launch before you start spending your time creating your content. Once you've made it to this step, you need to figure out an outline for your course. This is a very important step because you need to know the start and finish and how you are going to get there.

If your course comes out feeling unstructured, then people are going to be less likely to buy anything else from you, and they definitely won't spread the word. Once you have an outline for your course, then you can start to record your content. This can be a video or just an audio recording, but most people will prefer to have something to watch instead of just listening to you talk. Having visuals to back up what you are talking about makes learning a lot easier.

6. Make sure you pick the best software tools.

This applies more to webinars than online courses. Online courses are static. You simply upload them to a site where people buy them and then use the prerecorded information. For a webinar, it tends to happen live, and you want to make sure that it actually works so that people can enjoy what you are sharing and it plays all the way through without freezing.

There are some free and paid tools out there, and unfortunately, there will be some trial and error with this. But, I can suggest giving ezTalks Webinar a try. It has a lot to offer and you won't be hit with a bunch of extra fees that some software has. You can also attract people to a paid webinar by starting out with some free webinars from time to time. During a free one, you can plug your paid one and ask them to sign up, and if you have enticed them enough, they will.

Selling courses and webinars can be a very lucrative method of making money through your blog and with your expertise. It will take a lot of work, but it is worth it in the long run. You may also need to invest in some recording and audio equipment in order to make high-quality videos. In the end, if you use the tips provided, you will make your money back and then some.

Proven Strategies: How One Man Makes $40k/Month Selling Info

To round out this chapter, we are going to look at how one man was able to sell products and make $40,000 each month. He has used other monetization methods as well, like affiliate marketing, blogging, and Kindle publishing, but selling products has made him the most money.

When he sells products online, he is able to funnel the traffic and visitors that his blog gets into the products. Instead of simply being an affiliate for another person and only getting a commission, he gets all of the profits and is able to continue expanding his own business instead of another person's business.

The product he makes most of his money on is a course that teaches people how to make money using Kindle. He funnels people into signing up for his classes through all of his other sources, like the people who read his books or those who read his blog. He also uses affiliate marketers to help send him business, and he pays them a commission. He sells his course through a website called ClickBank, which also has its own affiliate marketing system. This isn't the only way to sell courses, though. Udemy is a popular place where people sell courses.

The man in this example explains that when he sells his course on different websites, like ClickBank, Udemy, and others, he tests different looks to see what works best. This is something that helps with every area of blogging. You want to attract people and not send them away, and having your site look nice as well as sharing enough information, helps to attract people. The man has found that placing a grid under his "buy" button with the recent purchases of his course has helped immensely.

Doing something like this, coming up with a course to sell that people find helpful and informative, will take time. For this particular businessman, it took him about six months to come up with his course. He also put $1000 into this course before he started seeing a return on his project. He suggests that people start out with selling Kindle books and being an affiliate marketer before trying to create a course like this.

Chapter 6: Blogging Secret #5: Advertising

We're going to round out this book by talking about advertising. This isn't advertising your blog, but instead, making money by placing ads on your blog. This is a very popular way to make money on blogs, and there are a lot of options, so everybody should be able to find a way to make money through advertisements.

Ads and Your Blog: Ways to Profit

The last way to monetize your blog that we are going to talk about, is through ads. Online advertising centers on three main forms of ads: pay-per-click, pay-per-impression, and pay-per-action.

Contextual ads are often pay-per-click. These ads are shared based on what you write about. In theory, the ads should match up with the content of your web page, which increases the odds of a person clicking on them. Google AdSense is the most popular version of this.

Text ads that use a hyperlink and are separate from the main content of the blog post – but which usually still have keywords matching the blog's theme – are known as text link ads.

Impression-based ads pay the blogger based on how many times their ad appears on their website.

Affiliate ads are ads that link people with relevant products on another website. The blogger gets paid when a reader clicks on the link and buys the product.

Then some bloggers use direct ads, which means they allow visitors to purchase ad space on their blog. These often show up as banners or other types of display ads. The pricing varies with each blogger.

Then you have sponsored reviews and sponsored posts. Reviews are indirect forms of ads. Companies will sometimes get in contact with a blogger to ask them for a review of their services, site, business, or product. Similar to this is the sponsored post. These line up with the content of a blog post, and are mentioned in a natural context. If a blogger is writing about baking, they may mention and share a link to their favorite mixer. The vendor will then pay the blogger for the mention.

All of the revenue from these various forms of advertising depends greatly on the traffic to your site. It is important that you have already worked hard to increase your traffic before you jump into ads, otherwise, you might be disappointed with what you make.

Direct Advertising: Mastering PPC, CPM, and More

Selling direct advertising is a solid way to bring in some money every month. This means that you place ads on your website for other sites, and they pay you to do so. There are many different forms of direct advertising that you can use, so the possibilities are endless. Now, before you start trying to make money going down this route, you want to make sure that you have enough readers. While there isn't a rule for how many you should have, try to shoot for around 50,000 page views before trying to sell ads.

There are six popular ways to make money through advertising:

- Paid reviews.

- Pop-ups.

- CPM ad networks.

- Sell text links.

- Sell your own ads.

- Pay per click.

1. Pay-per-click.

This is probably the most popular form of advertising. Pay-per-click, or PPC, or cost-per-click, or CPC, is an ad on your site that people have to click on. When they click on it, the advertiser will pay you an agreed-upon price. There are several websites that you can use to find ads.

Infolinks offers people a 70% revenue share and uses a PPC model. The in-text ads placed on your site are double-underlined words that will appear as ads when a person clicks on them. Infolinks also has InFrame, InTag, and InSearch ads. It offers payment options through Western Union and wire transfer once you reach $100, or through eCheck or PayPal once you reach $50.

Media.net is another option and is controlled by the Yahoo Bing Network. The ads that are placed focus on relevant keywords, so it will take some time before they match up well with your site. The more you use this platform, the better the algorithm will figure out the best keywords for your readers. Media.net also provides a dedicated account rep who can suggest more ways to increase your revenue through ads, and it uses PayPal or a wire transfer, with the payment minimum $100.

Chitika is another alternative for contextual ads and it offers a CPC program. The ads can be customized and they work well along with AdSense. The minimum payout is $10 through PayPal.

2. Sell ads.

You can sell direct ads on your blog and it places the control in your hands. The only thing you have to do is place an "Advertise With Us" page on your website and share the different types of formats of ads that you have available and how much it will cost them each month. You should also share your Google PageRank, Alexa rank, and any other traffic stats. But, you can save yourself the hassle of selling and use third-party alternatives.

BuySellAds is an ad-marketplace where people can place ad space for others to buy. You have to be a high traffic blog to post on this site, so if you are starting out, you will want to wait a few months.

3. Sell text links.

If your blog gets a lot of good organic traffic, you could try your hand at text-link ads. This is where you link a piece of text in your post to a page on another site. Before you start doing this, you should use a Nofollow tag to avoid a Google penalty.

LinkWorth is a text-link network where you will find options for paid reviews, text ads, and more.

4. Cost-per-click networks.

For the most part, we have covered the CPC model for ads. This means that you only get paid for ads if somebody clicks through. There is an alternative to this known as CPM, meaning cost per thousand, where you get paid for every 1000 impressions the ad gets. When it comes to CPC, the income can vary, but that doesn't happen with CPM. If the network sets the CPM at $5 then you will end up making $500 per 100,000 impressions, and so forth.

PulsePoint is a CPM network where you have the ability to set your price. To get accepted, you have to have a lot of original content. PulsePoint mainly sells to US-based viewers. When you come up with your price, make sure it is more than what you make with your backup. If they aren't able to pay what your backup pays you, then the backup is shown.

5. Pop-ups.

Most bloggers and advertisers steer clear of pop-up ads nowadays, but it is still an option. You can use pop-ups or pop-unders. A site you can use is called PopAds, and you can set your price and the frequency in which they happen for your visitors.

6. Paid reviews.

A decent amount of money can be made through publishing reviews for services and products that you trust and fit in your niche. The great thing about this is you get paid per review. Prices typically range from $150 to $500, but it all depends on your rank and traffic.

SponsoredReviews is a site that gives advertisers a chance to generate backlinks and a chance for bloggers to make money.

Some of these direct advertising options aren't even ads at all and are just sponsored reviews and posts. These are just a few ways to make money on your blog through advertising.

Become an AdSense Ninja

One of the most popular ways to start monetizing websites and blogs is through Google AdSense. AdSense basically gives the blogger a chance to add different ads to their site. When readers go to their blog and then click on an ad, the blogger makes money. Google will also take a little for themselves and then it sends out what is left to the blogger once a month. It is a very interesting way to make a little more money with your blog, but when you have the right-sized audience, AdSense can turn blogs into careers. But how can you be successful with this?

We're going to look at some ways to increase the revenue you make through Google AdSense, so that you can continue to make revenue throughout the life of your blog. We'll also round out this section by looking at ethical uses of contextual advertising, because using these ads ethically is just as important as using them correctly.

1. Properly place your ads.

The biggest problem people normally have when they first start out using AdSense is that they don't have a clue as to how to properly place the advertisements. There are a lot of different factors that you have to remember when it comes to ad placement.

First off, you should make sure that your ads are placed where your visitors will see them right off the bat. However, you need to make sure you balance out the number of ads so that they don't come off as annoying. Nobody likes going to those websites that have so many ads that it slows down the site and it's hard to find the actual content.

Typically, good ad placement will begin with placing a single long rectangular ad. You can also place a couple of ads on the right of the page for visibility. These ads can be 160 by 600 to 300 by 250. You can play around with the numbers within acceptable ranges to figure out what is best for you. Again, you have to make sure that you don't overdo things with the number of ads. Not only are your visitors going to get annoyed, but the more ads you have on your page, the less money you will make with each click. So, fewer ads mean that you could make more money.

2. Try to use high paying keywords.

Nearly every single niche within the accepted topics of Google will have "high paying" keywords. There are some topics that Google excludes in its AdSense, like tobacco. When you use high paying keywords within your article for your niche, you are going to receive ads that fit within that. When you have ads that match up to good keywords, you will make more revenue and get more clicks.

Figuring out what these high paying keywords are is easy. Google offers a keyword planner tool that is free to use and will give you the chance to search for several different phrases, keywords, or websites and figure out what keywords readers are looking for. You can also sort the information out by price so that you know which one makes the most money per click.

As you start working with different keywords you will start to learn what works best for your niche. There will be a lot of trial and error when you first start out because keywords and ads work together. As you start using different keywords, your ads will change as well.

You may find that you receive more clicks with lower value keywords, or might make more money by using the top keyword. Like with everything else, it will require tweaks as you start to develop your blog and use ads.

3. Change up the design of the ads.

After you have figured out the ads you will use, you can edit them in order to make them fit on your site. You shouldn't skip this when incorporating ads. Your ads should never stick out like a sore thumb. There are a few things to take into consideration when doing this. First, you want to make sure that you use colors and borders that match up with your website.

Then you should make sure that you use complimenting colors in the text and background of your ads. They need to stick out, but it shouldn't be in a glaring way. You want them to be clear and noticeable. If your website has a dark background, then you should use a lighter color so that the ad is noticeable. You should always do a preview to see if the ad looks natural.

4. Keep an eye on your results.

Too many people will upload some ads to their AdSense account and then forget about them. They don't check in on them each day, or even once a week. They just sit around and wait for money to come in at the end of each month. You can't make a decent amount of money if you don't check in on the ads to see if they are working for you. AdSense gives you the ability to track analytics on your ads to see what is working and what could use some improvement.

You should think about using a form of A/B testing. For example, on one of your blogs, you could place two ads and then three on another blog post. Then you can check in on the results each day to see which way is working better. If you discover that the post with three ads is working better for you, come up with another blog using three ads. Check to see if that blog gets consistent results. You then will need to continue to edit and tweak your ads until you like the money that you are making on your pages.

The sky's the limit when it comes to working with AdSense. Google provides bloggers with everything they need in order to be successful. If you also use other blogging tools, such as a lead list where you send out content, make sure you monitor the clicks you are getting on your ads regularly, and update those ads so that they will blend seamlessly into your site. There isn't a limit to how much you can make using AdSense.

Ethical Contextual Advertising

Knowing the best way to place ads on your site is one thing, but ethically using ads is another. This may sound like something I made up, or that it's not important, but you'd be surprised how often bloggers use some shady ad placement tactics. These tactics will also cost you readers and money. First off, let's quickly go over the four types of contextual ads that you can pick from:

- **Textual**: these are ads that link to other web resources without using modal pop-ups.

- **Pop-up**: these are ads that show a modal pop-up when the mouse moves over them.

- **Banner**: these are video, animated, or static ads that are placed in your posts.

- **Affiliate**: these are banner or textual ads that have affiliate codes in them that you earn a commission on when somebody places a purchase after clicking through.

All four of these types of ads can be used on your website if you would like. But we're here to talk about the rough side of content links, and these options have to be handled with care. This will help you to make some important decisions about the best display practices.

1. Privacy friendly or intrusive?

Script-based, dynamic ads like the ones provided by Chitika, Kontera, and InfoLinks are often intrusive to the privacy of the user because that not only tracks the clicks but the browsing activities and behavior of the user across your website and other web pages. Static links don't track users and are more privacy-friendly. Even if they do track, it is limited to the clicks and where they lead. There are two rules you should try to follow:

> • Make sure that users give you "permission" to use dynamic ads, because this will make them more likely to accept the ads you have and they will feel as if you are trustworthy. This can be done through polls on your blog, mailing list, or modal dialogs that ask the readers if they want to enable ads.

> • When using static links, place them where they make the most sense with your content and then diversify them through custom CSS so they don't look like your regular links.

Whatever you decide to do, make sure that you have a privacy policy where your users know what type of ads you have on your blog and let them know what the risks are for loading, viewing, and clicking on the ads.

2. Disclosure.

This tends to not be an issue for dynamic ads. The dynamic ad systems will normally automatically diversify ads from the regular links on a website. If your regular links are blue, then the system doing the dynamic ads may make them orange. When it comes to static links, it works a bit differently. The banners don't come with a disclosure. Plus, AdBlock won't recognize static banner ads as ads since they aren't script-based.

So, while dynamic ads come with their own style and a third-party disclosure, static ads will require you to add these things manually. You will need CSS styling to make them stand out from your other graphics and links. You will also need disclaimers on every page with these ads letting your readers know that there are ads on your site and what that means.

Not marking sponsored content, you will push your readers away, because they will feel as if they can't trust you. There are also laws that state that all advertising relationships have to be shared with the public.

3. Ad-blocker problems.

Business Insider released a report on ad-blocking in 2015 and it stated the number of ad-blocking users around the world had grown from 121 million to 181 million in a single year. This is a trend that worries the publishing and advertising industry. But viewers started doing this for a reason. Ad-blocking became more popular because websites had started to abuse the experience of the viewer. Nobody likes to be bombarded by pop-ups as soon as they visit a website.

I would suggest that you think about the types of ads that you are going to use and the reason why your viewers may choose to block them. The best way to figure out what your viewers would be okay with is to create a poll or survey and ask them if they are afraid of ads or they have ever clicked on a malicious ad.

If you choose to use dynamic ads, then you could use a cookie-based disclaimer that notices ad-blockers and shows a message to the viewer if they will allow ads on your website. If you have a WordPress-based blog, there is a plugin that you can use known as AdBlock Alerter that will do all of this for you.

To work around this problem altogether, you can choose to go with static ads with counters. This works for affiliate links and it won't trigger ad-blocking software.

4. Contextual ads and guest posts

Yes, ads should be used in your posts and guest posts, but you will need to figure out which, dynamic or static, will work best. Let's say you choose to use static ads and let's say that you let your guest bloggers include some products or affiliate links within their post. When you get asked to place a link to that post that matches the keywords of the writer, and the link takes the viewers to a competitor of the writer's brand, that writer will likely end up feeling betrayed and it could hurt your relationship with them. This is something you want to avoid.

If you want to use static ads, you will want to speak with the writer of the post first, letting them know and then ask if any conflict could arise. No matter what their answer is, you will have proven to the writer that you are trustworthy and they may end up writing more posts.

Dynamic ads put links into your posts automatically, so unless you add a "Guest Post" section and exclude that section from ads, or you reject the link, there is nothing that you can do. However, guest bloggers will likely already know that they are contributing to a site that uses dynamic ads. If, for some reason, they are not aware of this, reach out to them and inform them. Basically, make sure that conflicts of interest don't come up.

Backlinking Secrets: Ways to Profit Without Begging

It can be very frustrating to try and develop backlinks to your website. It is a process that requires dedication, patience, and work. We are no longer in the days of simple SEO where you can add any type of link into your site anywhere on the internet. In order for backlinks to be successful, copywriters and digital marketers have to be conscious of their backlink strategy.

Backlinks are one of the most traditional SEO techniques and they provide an easy way to increase search rankings and traffic. However, you only need high-quality links in order to generate the best SEO results and to boost your site traffic.

Ever since backlinks have become one of the most popular ways to boost a website's SEO ranking, Google has switched up its classification for backlinks and how they affect a site's rankings. So, nowadays, in order to build backlinks, site managers and owners have to make sure that they work to organically grow backlinks with time.

To simply explain backlinks, they are also known as external backlinks and they are another site owners link to a different person's website. They could place this link on a service page, a blog post, or some other place on their site. Backlinks are very important for SEO because the number of quality backlinks that your site has helps to back up the content quality on your site.

Backlinks play a very important role for end users and search engines. For search engines, they help them to figure out how relevant and authoritative your site is to your topic. Backlinks also send a signal to search engines that there are other sites who are endorsing your work. If there are a lot of sites that link to the same site or page, search engines learn that the content is worth sharing a link to, and as such, they rank the site higher on the results page. For a long time, the number of backlinks helped to show the popularity of a page, but today, we have different algorithms. These new algorithms were made to help determine other ranking factors. Pages will rank higher depending on the quality of the links that other sites are giving them instead of the quantity.

As for end-users, backlinks connect them with information that is close to what has been written by other sites. Backlinks work like a connection point for information that a reader may want to check out. It gives them a solid experience because it sends them directly to other desirable information.

While it is pretty much impossible to know the algorithm that is used by Google and other search engines to qualify content, there are some good ideas for site managers and owners to use to help improve their rankings and to create genuine backlinks.

What you can do is use the following tricks and tips in order to create backlinks without having to beg other people. These will help you to grow your online presence:

1. Let other bloggers credit the work they have done for you.

Everybody wants to create a portfolio in order to showcase their best work; whether they are business owners, entrepreneurs, copywriters, web designers and so on. Most of the time, these portfolios will also have some kind of backlink to other sites so that their viewers can review the work of their service provider.

Not only will allowing backlinks from portfolios help to improve the other person's business, but it will also place you higher within the search rankings for Google.

2. Talk to an influencer.

Using influencers as a marketing tactic is very popular right now. A lot of brands want to know how to get an athlete or celebrity to endorse their work, or become business partners with them. But you can do things a different way. You can choose to interview influencers in order to gain knowledge from them that could help your audience.

If you have yet to build connections to some influencers, you will need to be really good at email outreach and have good people skills. If you get the interview, it is very important to make sure that you have some thoughtful questions put together, and that you respect the person's time. Most people will want to keep the interview under 15 minutes, but if you know what you want to ask and have spent some time coming up with good questions, then you should be able to get plenty of insight during that time. Your interview can be published as a video or a transcript.

3. Create content that is shareable.

Shareable content is simple content that can be shared, which provides you with the chance to have your work shared throughout the internet and ups your odds of having your site linked to multiple platforms and web pages. Whether you choose to come up with well-researched blog posts, infographics, or actionable e-books, any content that is shared can be distributed through a call-to-action asking your readers to share the information any way they want to.

Pinterest, the often forgotten social media platform, is a great way to get backlinks. It's important that you make sure that your highly valuable content, infographics, case studies, and blog posts, are linked to a board on your Pinterest. If somebody finds your information helpful, there is a good chance that they will end up creating a backlink when they post the content on their website.

Your initial reach can easily be done through social media, hashtags, and other types of targeted distribution in order to get your work to others within your chosen niche.

4. Come up with a quiz.

Quizzes are very popular and they tend to be shared a lot. If you create a quiz for your site, you can embed it and get backlinks like you do when you have infographics. You need to make sure that your quizzes are fun. You don't have to make them be a knowledge test. It is a good idea to make quizzes that will encourage people to look inward and think about who they are; the result they get will then be something they want to share. This is something that Buzzfeed has capitalized on.

5. Use backlinks on your website.

Another way to make sure that you create shareable content is to create well-researched posts that link your readers to other important content within your niche. For example, you could come up with countdown posts to your top travel blogs so that you can link to other popular websites, and this creates an opportunity for that popular site to share your work and then create a link back to your site.

All of this means that you need to make sure you put your best foot forward when you are trying to generate backlinks, so it is important that you give shout-outs to the content creators, services, or products that make your life better.

You could also decide to do some sort of content round-up to bring together helpful tricks and tips for a specific concept or topic. If you want to do something like this, using Feedly can help you out. Feedly gives you the ability to find posts and articles that relate to certain topics. Coming up with a content round-up once a week will keep your readers updated on what they find important, and you should always link back to every website that you mention.

6. Share testimonials.

When you provide free testimonials, it is a win-win for everybody. The person you share a testimonial about gets free publicity and you also get your company and name shared on their site, as well as a backlink. Obviously, you should make sure that you are an actual customer of the company. You should never share a testimonial for a company or product you have never used.

7. Write guest posts for other sites.

Guest posts are at the top of the list for ways to showcase your expertise and generate backlinks. The majority of blogs and websites will have a short biography at the top or bottom of the posts, which will give you a space for a backlink.

Not only will doing these guest posts give you the chance to show off your knowledge, but working with other people will help you to build your professional rapport and create a brand personality. It can be hard to get up the nerve to reach out to other websites, but it is worth it if they do agree to post your guest post.

8. Do more online networking.

Whether you're a business owner or online entrepreneur, you have probably been informed more than once that networking is the key to business success. Networking has now made it to the digital realm using sites like Facebook and LinkedIn for business. Networking now has more benefits than ever before, with new opportunities to pitch guest posts, share content, and agree to add backlinks to sites of people who you have created a close professional relationship with.

Networking is great for everybody involved, and it gives you the chance to work on your professional communication abilities and business-building strategies.

9. Get more creative.

If you want to generate backlinks faster, then you need to get more creative. Having plenty of shareable content is a high-value, high-return endeavor, so why shouldn't you use some creativity in order to begin a new project to form some backlinks?

Using your various social media platforms to link to your site is extremely helpful, but this should be used sparingly. Don't link to your website with every single post. If you are an expert, then why shouldn't you share some of the work that you have done for other people? Reports and case studies about past work or customer experiences should and can be freely shared within your social media world, and it will demonstrate your value and expertise to future customers.

Much in the same way that you allow your digital service providers and designers to promote work they have done for you, you can also ask your clients to share what you have created for them. Case studies can also be very helpful when you want to land a guest post deal with a major website, as it lets them know that you care about what you are doing and are proud of it.

10. Collaborate with others on projects.

Using collaboration within a creative endeavor is always a great way to generate backlinks and to reach a larger audience. Things like podcasts have become more and more popular with business owners and creatives. This is because it gives them the chance to share their expertise while also linking back to their site in the episode description.

11. Make sure you stick to your niche.

Exchanging backlinks and networking can bring everybody immense rewards, but only if things are done correctly. You need to make sure that you take some time to get to know the other person, their business, and how your work can fit into their site. For example, you shouldn't worry about sharing in-depth case studies on coaching people on leadership development if direct ties don't exist.

It is important to stick with your niche when it comes to generating backlinks, so you need to make sure that your link sharing matches up with your niche so that you have a clean "record" because this will help with your rankings.

12. Get interviewed and perform interviews.

It doesn't matter what industry you are in, interviews are done regularly to create shareable content. If you are great at public speaking or you have the time to come up with a thoughtful reply to interview questions, this can help to improve your number of backlinks.

The main thing you need to remember when generating backlinks is making sure that each website that links to you is just as dedicated to sharing quality content as you are. While we are unsure of the criterion that classifies a site as "quality," it is very impressive what a few high-value backlinks are able to do with your rankings.

Trying to come up with backlinks is tedious, but if you are serious about your blogging and generating good backlinks on several accounts and websites within your niche, you will be able to stay high up in the ranks with Google and keep traffic coming to your site.

Remember that your content and website quality goes a long way in creating relationships and professional rapport with others who may backlink to your site. You want to make sure that your content is always actionable and useful; that it targets high-rated sites; and that you constantly nurture your online relationships to get the backlinks that will positively affect your rankings.

Proven Strategies: Google AdSense Earns This Blogger $800/Week

It might be all fine and dandy to hear how you can use AdSense to improve your blog and make it profitable, but it means nothing if you don't have proof to back it up. So that's what this last section is going to do. I'm going to share with you a true story about a man who was able to use Google AdSense to bring in around $800 each week.

This blogger receives most of his blog traffic from Facebook. He is a niche blogger, and one of his best days with Google AdSense made him close to $200. The main reason for this was because his post went viral on Facebook. According to him, 85% of his blog traffic comes from Facebook and the rest comes from email marketing.

While he does make a lot of money through Facebook itself, we are going to talk about how he also monetizes with Google AdSense. While Google doesn't bring in as much money as Facebook does, because it is pay per click, it does bring in quite a bit per week. In fact, it probably brings him more per week than most people's jobs pay them.

Google AdSense is one of the simplest things that you can start monetizing your website with. Even when you are only getting 1000 to 2000 people to your blog each day, it can still sometimes provide you with around $20 a day. Now, in this success story we're talking about, the blogger is driving traffic to his blog through email marketing, Facebook, and several other sources.

The way he ensures he makes his money through AdSense is to make sure that he focuses his traffic on the United States. The US tends to have more clicks on the ads and it has the highest pay rate. While many people say in order to be profitable with Google AdSense you have to rank high on Google, this blogger says that's not necessarily true. Ranking on Google can help you earn more revenue with AdSense, but according to the man in our example, as long as you have a good email list, you shouldn't have a problem with earning AdSense revenue.

To make sure that he makes the most money possible with AdSense and his other revenue options, he has blogs that require daily content. This means that he is sending things out to his followers every single day, which means that people are receiving updates from him every day. This ensures that nobody ever forgets about his site and there is somebody on the website each day.

For the blog, he shares news each day. This can be done in almost every niche. For example, if you have a sports blog, you can easily share news about UFC, or whatever sport you blog about. The man also explained that in order to get to where he is today, he had to invest a bit of money into driving traffic to his sites. He used Facebook ads, and by doing this, he was able to capture email addresses and subscribers. Then he could send them updates about new posts whenever he wanted.

This blogger believes the reason that he is so successful is that he has picked a niche that requires daily content. He explained that all other big blogs like Buzzfeed started out being run by a daily blogger. By making sure you have something to share every day that will drive high-quality traffic, then you are well on your way to succeeding. Daily news content that fits with your niche is one of the best ways to build up an audience quickly.

He also talks about how investing some money into his blog has helped him. He bought content and pays around $200 or more each month for a website hosting account that will ensure the site runs smoothly with a lot of traffic. He also spent $10 to $15 each day on posts to help drive traffic to the ads, but he said you don't have to do this; it's just what he chose to do. Once he got his audience up to 10,000 to 15,000 people, his audience started to grow by itself and he stopped having to pay for traffic.

The man ends his advice by saying that the $800 he makes each week with AdSense comes from two blogs that he has on one AdSense account.

But, throughout this blogger's whole story about how he makes upwards of $800 each week with AdSense, he kept saying that he monetized his sites in other ways as well. Relying solely on AdSense is not the best idea, because it requires clicks and it requires people to be on a PC. It doesn't work as well for mobile users. That said, you should still use AdSense. It is a great revenue option and will bring in more money.

Conclusion

Thank you for making it through to the end of *Blogging: Unlock the Secrets to Making Your Blog Posts into Profit and Discover How Bloggers Make Money Online Utilizing Affiliate Marketing and Other E-Commerce Skills for Passive Income*. It should have been informative and provided you with all of the tools you need to achieve your goals: whatever they may be.

The next step is to use the information you have learned within this book. While there may be a lot to it, the easiest place to start is with your niche. You can't start blogging until you know what you want to blog about. Figure out your niche and then start looking at what other people are doing in that area. Use that information to learn how you can make it better, and then move onto creating your blog. Once you feel comfortable with your blog and you have begun to post regularly and attracted some loyal readers, you can start to branch out in other ways, like e-commerce or creating informative products like an online class.

While you are doing all of this, you still need to remember to keep an eye on your analytics and use advertising. These are how you will make sure you keep your information in line with your competition and continue bringing in more and more readers. With the right approach, you can succeed and profit from your blog.

Finally, if you found this book useful in any way, a review on Amazon is always appreciated!

Check out another book by Matthew Shields

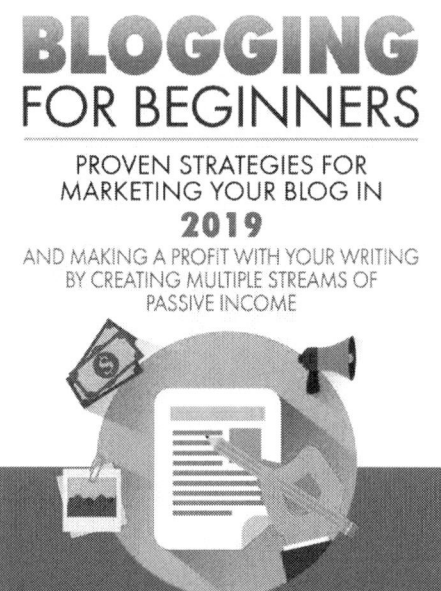

Printed in Great Britain
by Amazon